President Eisenhower signs — on January 3, 1959 — the proclamation admitting Alaska as the 49th State. Witnessing the signing are from left to right: Representative Ralph J. Rivers, Senator Ernest Gruening, Senator E. L. (Bob) Bartlett, Secretary of the Interior Fred A. Seaton, Acting Governor of Alaska Waino Hendrickson, David W. Kendall, special counsel to the President, Mike Stepovich, former Governor of Alaska, Robert B. Atwood, Editor and Publisher of Anchorage Times.

Photo by Tom Abercrombie, courtesy of National Geographic Magazine.

The Battle for Alaska Statehood

by *Ernest Gruening, U. S. S.*

Published by
The University of Alaska Press
College, Alaska
in cooperation with
The Alaska Purchase Centennial Commission

Distributed by
The University of Washington Press
Seattle and London

F
909
G88

55292

Dedication

T O Bob Bartlett, who, as Alaska's
Delegate to Congress from 1945
to 1959, and as the Territory's sole legislative representative in the nation's
capital from the time Alaskans declared
they wanted statehood, brought their
aspiration to fulfillment by making
Alaska the 49th State; and

To the people of Alaska, whose wisdom
and determination made that achievement possible.

Foreword

THIS history, commemorating the 100th anniversary of Alaska's purchase from Russia in 1867, is the second of a series of historical papers to be published by the Alaska Purchase Centennial Commission with the cooperation of the University of Alaska Press.

The author, U.S. Senator Ernest Gruening, is eminently qualified to tell the story of Alaska's battle for statehood. After receiving a medical degree in 1912 he became a journalist and had a distinguished career in that field until 1933. In 1933 he was appointed by President Franklin D. Roosevelt as adviser to the United States Delegation to the Seventh Inter-American Conference at Montevideo, and in 1934 became Director of the Division of Territories and Island Possessions. Since then he has been intimately involved in the affairs of Alaska.

From 1939 to 1953 he served as Governor of Alaska, and in 1953-1954 he wrote The State of Alaska, a book which was destined to have profound effect on the course of Alaska's history.

In 1955 he delivered the keynote address to the Alaska Constitutional Convention, and in 1956 he and William A. Egan were elected provisionally to the United States Senate under the Alaska-Tennessee Plan to work for statehood in the Congress.

Statehood was achieved in 1958, and Ernest Gruening was elected to the United States Senate. He is currently serving his second term as a United States Senator from Alaska.

In this book the Senator, always a central figure and keen observer in the long battle to achieve statehood, dramatically tells the story of that battle.

B. G. Olson
Executive Editor
Alaska Purchase Centennial
Commission Publications Board

Introduction

Some months ago I was asked to write an account of our statehood fight to be published in the Centennial Year as a joint project of the University of Alaska and Alaska's Purchase Centennial Commission. This was a fascinating assignment, which I accepted as a labor of love, perhaps unthinkingly and without an immediate realization of the scope that such a work should properly have, and of the problem of adding this to my other duties.

At the time, my conversations with B. G. Olson at the University, who was in charge of this project, indicated that there would be several contributors, primarily those who had taken a major part in the statehood fight: Bob Bartlett, of course, who was our Delegate during all those years from the real initiation of the final statehood drive in the middle '40's, when he took over the torch from Tony Dimond, to its successful conclusion in 1959—years in which he carried the entire Congressional legislative burden, not merely for statehood, but for all other Alaskan concerns; William A. Egan, Governor, pioneer in an effort to introduce statehood legislation on the Territorial level in his first session in the Alaska Legislature in 1941, an attempt which failed only because he was a little ahead of his time and his fellow-legislators were not as advanced on that issue as he was;[1] and Ralph Rivers, who, along with Bill Egan and me, constituted the Alaska-Tennessee Plan delegation in Congress and, prior to that, as Territorial Attorney-General, had served most helpfully in drafting revenue and other legislation for our Territory which would be instrumental in approaching our statehood goals.

With this presumed division of labor, it seemed to me that while as inclusive as possible within limitations of time and space of all statehood activities, each contributor should concentrate particularly on his own activities. This I have attempted to do. It should be clear, however, that no one person, and no two or three or half a dozen persons, can be credited with the achievement of statehood for Alaska, whatever might have been their individual efforts. The credit belongs to all the people of Alaska, who, in varying degrees and to the full extent of their powers and opportunities, backed the battle to achieve for Alaska, long-neglected stepchild in the national family, the realization of that most basic of American principles—government by consent of the governed.

One individual, however, not an Alaskan, I think, deserves to be especially saluted. He is Harry S Truman, who responded immediately in the earliest days of his Presidency to the plea that he support statehood, even in advance of the time that the people of Alaska had, through referendum, declared their desire for it, and continued unceasingly during the remainder of his Presidential term to support and encourage that objective. He was the first and only President to do so.

Finally, it is clear to me that the definitive account of the battle for Alaskan statehood remains to be written, and should be. It would, and should, require a vast amount of painstaking research to which I have not been able to give the time. An important part of that research would deal with the earlier pro-statehood efforts, especially of Delegate James Wickersham, who introduced the first Statehood Bill on March 30, 1916, by an odd coincidence on the 49th anniversary of the signing of the Treaty of Cession; with the subsequent efforts of Delegate Anthony J. Dimond; and with the admirable labors of the Alaska Constitutional Convention and with the collateral efforts to secure statehood for our sister Pacific State, Hawaii, whose story is at various times and points closely intertwined with our own and has heroic aspects which should be immortalized. Together, their efforts inscribed two additional and inspiring verses in the American Epic, for together we extended the frontiers of freedom and democracy to America's farthest North, West and South, and ringingly reaffirmed our historic professions of liberty and equality.

Governor Gruening thanking President Harry S. Truman for his support of the Alaska statehood cause.

Prologue

MY concern for Alaskan statehood doubtless had its origins on September 15, 1934, when I went to Hyde Park, New York, to see President Roosevelt. I was taken there by Oscar L. Chapman, Assistant Secretary of the Interior, who had urged my appointment to a new post created by Executive Order of the President. The position was that of Director of the Division of Territories and Island Possessions in the Department of the Interior. It was projected by President Roosevelt as a supervisory agency over the Federal relations of our outlying areas, which at that time included Alaska, Hawaii, Puerto Rico, and the Virgin Islands, and subsequently, the Philippines. My visit to Hyde Park was for the purpose of receiving President Roosevelt's views on the conduct of this new agency which I was to head.

While designed to supervise the Federal relations, another aspect in the President's mind, I learned from him, was that it should assist these politically underprivileged areas—underprivileged because they had no voting representation in the Congress—in whatever way such an agency might assist them to compensate for this lack of voting representation. There was a prospect, also, that other areas then under the control of the Navy, such as Samoa and Guam, would be added, as they since have been. Subsequently, also the Antarctic Service was added to the responsibilities of the Division of Territories, and I was delegated by President Roosevelt as Chairman of a committee of four, with a representative from the Coast Guard, one from the Navy, and one from the State Department, to organize the first government expedition to Antarctica in 1938. I did so, and our United States permanent program of research in Antarctica was thereby established.

When we arrived at Hyde Park, the President was in earnest conference with Harry Hopkins, the Director of the W.P.A., and Rexford Guy Tugwell, one of the so-called brain-trusters who became Under Secretary of Agriculture. They were discussing the desirability of shelter belts of trees in the prairie states. After we listened to the discussion for awhile, the President turned to me and said: "Now, about the territories." He outlined what he hoped would be the beneficial accomplishments of this new agency and then reviewed, in summary, what he felt were the needs of each of the outlying areas. Of Alaska, he said: "Alaska needs more people and we ought to do something to stimulate agriculture there. Next year I would like to have you move 1,000 or 1,500 people from the drought-stricken agricultural areas in the Middle West and see if we cannot give them a new start in life in Alaska." This was the mandate which developed into the Matanuska Valley colonization project, and was initiated the following Spring; but that is another story.

In the course of our conversation, I said to President Roosevelt: "Isn't this new agency the equivalent of the British Colonial Office?" He said: "I suppose it is." I commented: "It seems to me that the United States shouldn't have any colonies." The President smiled and extended his hands, palms upward, in a gesture, saying: "Well, I think you're right. Let's see what you can develop." Nothing more definite was said at the time, but it seemed to me an indication that I was at least to explore the possibilities of getting rid of the colonial status which these wards of the United States then had.

DURING my five years as Director of Territories, I visited Alaska—in 1936 and 1938 (this was before Alaska could be reached by air)—and sought to become familiar with its problems and needs. But it was not until my appointment as Governor in 1939, after John W. Troy, who had been appointed at the beginning of the Roosevelt administration, had resigned, that I was able to come to grips with some of the realities.

One of these was the realization that the revenues derived from Alaska's resources were virtually negligible. Alaska was in the grip of absentee interests and had been for a quarter of a century. They were violently opposed to any taxation that would lessen their profits or in any way interfere with their desire to take as much from Alaska as quickly as possible. At that time, whole categories of businesses paid no taxes whatever to the Territory. These included banks, newspapers, radio stations, filling stations and garages, logging operations, motion picture theatres, bus, air and steamship lines, lighterage companies, light and power companies, construction companies and building contractors, etc., etc. The tax on the great bounty derived from our abundant fishery resources by the absentee interests which processed them was negligible. So were the taxes on mining operations. No property taxes were levied outside of municipalities. The thousands of non-residents who came up from "down below" every Spring to fish, engage in placer mining or construction and went back in the Fall well-heeled, often to the extent of thousands of dollars for their season's work, paid only a $5.00 so-called "school tax". The wealth of Alaska was being drained off and next to nothing was staying there for its needs. It was clear that whatever might be the future of Alaska, revenues were required to take care of the Territory's public services—education, health, highways, municipal functions, etc. At that time there wasn't even a Department of Health, as such, although the incidence of tuberculosis among our Native population was nine times what it was in the States.

Although I had taken the oath of office in December of 1939, the first legislature thereafter would not convene until early in 1941. Meanwhile, I had explored the possibility of revenue legislation with the prospective members of that legislature and found, what seemed to me, general receptiveness for this idea. I undoubtedly was naive about their assurances and didn't realize the power of the lobby of the absentee interests, chiefly those of canned salmon, mining and maritime transportation. So, an income tax I proposed to the 1941 Legislature got nowhere, as did most of my proposals at that session. I met the situation by issuing a message to the people of

Alaska after the session, giving them my views, which were decidedly critical as to its performance—a practice I followed thereafter.

By 1945 I realized that Alaska's territorial status burdened it with insuperable handicaps and that statehood was essential. But it was necessary first to get an official pronouncement from the people of Alaska to determine whether they really wanted it. So, in my Message to the 1945 Legislature, I recommended that a provision for a referendum on statehood be enacted to take place at the coming election in the Fall of 1946. It was enacted.

Meanwhile, a pro-statehood resolution, sponsored by Stanley J. McCutcheon, of Anchorage, and Fred Hanford, of Wrangell, was also adopted by the 1945 legislature.

In April of 1945, President Roosevelt died and was succeeded by Harry S Truman. President Truman had sent out a general invitation to all Governors to come and see him and discuss their problems, and I took advantage of this invitation when he was on the West Coast visiting his friend, Governor Mon Wallgren, of Washington, at his residence at Olympia. At this meeting, I informed the President of the action of the 1945 Territorial legislature in providing a statehood referendum, and asked him whether he could see his way clear, in his first State of the Union Message, which would take place the following January, to give Alaskan statehood a plug. He agreed, and did so. This was what he said in that message:

> "The major governments of the world face few problems as important and as perplexing as those relating to dependent peoples. This Government is committed to the democratic "principle that it is for the dependent people themselves to decide what their status shall be. To this end I asked the Congress last October to provide a means by which the people of Puerto Rico might choose their form of government and ultimate status with respect to the United States. I urge, too, that the Congress promptly accede to the wishes of the people of Hawaii that the Territory be admitted to statehood in our Union, and that similar action be taken with respect to Alaska as soon as it is certain that this is the desire of the people of that great Territory."

At the 1946 election, the people of Alaska voted that they wanted statehood by a vote of 9,630 to 6,822. While the majority was not overwhelming, the three to two vote was understandable because of the long-standing opposition propaganda of the really controlling forces—the absentee interests.

A majority of the Territory's newspapers at that time opposed statehood. The paper in Juneau—the Daily Alaska Empire—directed by former Governor Troy's daughter, Mrs. Helen Monsen, was violently opposed to it. So was the Fairbanks News-Miner, owned and operated by Austin E. Lathrop, the Territory's leading industrialist and the Republican National Committeeman. Likewise was one of the two newspapers in Ketchikan, the Fishing News, controlled by the absentee salmon interests, and one of the two in Anchorage, The News. (Subsequently, under different ownerships or changed conditions, their opposition to statehood ceased.)[1]

Also, there was the realization of many people of Alaska that there could be no statehood until we had a revenue system and were able to support ourselves with the added requirements of statehood.

I continued to work for such a system, with only little success, although the 1945 legislature, in response to my requests, did put through some important measures, such as a Development Board, a Housing Authority, a Department of Agriculture, a full-time Commissioner of Health, an enlarged Department of Labor, an anti-discrimination bill to make racial discrimination against our aboriginal population, Indians and Eskimos, a misdemeanor, a teachers' retirement act, and a bill prohibiting billboards on highways. Because it failed to enact Veterans' legislation, I had requested, I called a special session early in 1946 and had aroused sufficient support so that the legislation was enacted. With subsequent amendments, it has been functioning effectively and beneficially ever since.

The legislature elected in 1946, however—which would be the 1947 legislature—and one that proved to be the worst legislature in my experience through its crude flouting of the public interest—really paved the way for a change. It saddled the Territory with four million dollars more of expenditures than it provided revenues. It made necessary for us to pass the hat to keep the University of Alaska open.

By this time, the people were aroused, and in the 1948 election, they made a clean sweep and prepared the way for the 1949 legislature, the best in Alaska's territorial history.[2] This legislature enacted a comprehensive revenue system—income tax, business license tax, a progressive trap tax, permissive sales taxes for municipalities and school districts, and various other useful measures, such as establishing a Territorial Department of Fisheries. While under the restrictions placed upon Alaska by the Organic Act of 1912, vesting control of our great fishery resources in the Federal Government, which was ruining them, this new Territorial agency had only advisory powers, it paved the way for the competent State agency that would come into being ten years later and would gradually overcome the depletion caused by the twenty-year mismanagement of the Fish and Wildlife Service.

Having received a mandate from the people of Alaska that they wanted statehood, I was free to work for it. As Governor of Alaska, it was necessary for me to go to Washington four or five times a year in order to appear before Congressional committees on Alaska's needs, and to assist our voteless delegate in Congress in presenting Alaska's requirements. On these trips, I would seek every opportunity to address groups on Alaska, when I would always stress the need and desirability of statehood. During the next twelve years, I talked to several hundred gatherings—universities and colleges, women's clubs, service clubs, veterans organizations, religious congregations, teachers' conventions, Chambers of Commerce, including the Chamber of Commerce of the United States, which I persuaded to endorse statehood, and to any and all who would listen. I could and did glowingly paint the great beauties of Alaska, its mountains rising from the sea, its virgin forests, its abundant wildlife, the charm of its unspoiled wilderness, the friendliness of its people, and their pioneer characteristics; but I would also point out the extent of the discriminations which Alaska suffered as a stepchild of the national family and that the only solution lay in statehood. Generally, there would be a question period. If one hadn't been planned, I would ask for one, and invariably the question would be asked how those present could help Alaska secure statehood. I would explain that statehood would come if, in any one Congress, a majority of both houses would enact a statehood bill, and urged those present, if they believed our cause to be just, to write to their respective Senators and Representatives. In addition to that, in every city that I visited to give these talks, I would make a point of calling on the newspaper editors. As an old newspaperman, as former Managing Editor of the New York Tribune and of the New York Post, of the Boston Traveler and Journal, and as a magazine editor, I had a ready entree to these sanctums. The editors were interested in Alaska, which always has had an aura of romance, and I think I performed a not too difficult selling job on the desirability of making Alaska a State. I am confident that my efforts were sufficiently successful so that in the closing days of our battle for statehood, there was only one major city newspaper—in Richmond, Virginia—where there was active editorial opposition to statehood. Public opinion increasingly favored it. In fact, as the Gallup Polls successively showed, the people of America were well ahead of the Congress in their support of Alaskan statehood.

Since Alaskans had voted that they wanted statehood, I conceived the idea that it would be helpful to get the support of the State Governors. There was a conference held of the Governors of the forty-eight states every year. These had been initiated by Theodore Roosevelt in 1908, to interest the Governors in conservation. They had somewhat later included the Governors of the two Pacific territories, Alaska and Hawaii, in their conference, and would add Puerto Rico and the Virgin Islands in the 1940's. But I had not attended the seven conferences from 1940 to 1946 inclusive. The reason for my non-attendance was that these conferences were held in June, a month in which leaving Alaska was most difficult. The highly seasonal factor in Alaska, as we all know, makes the Summer months the period of maximum activity. Everything begins to happen in May and continues through September—fishing, placer mining, construction, tourism, etc. This was the period when V.I.P.'s visited Alaska and hardly the time when the Governor should absent himself. So, I passed up the first seven conferences after I became Governor, little appreciating what delightful occasions they were apart from the opportunity of learning from other Governors how they met their problems and exchanging views with them.

But, after the Alaskans' favorable vote on statehood in the 1946 referendum, I felt I should go to the next Governors' Conference and see whether I could not persuade the State Governors to adopt a resolution supporting statehood for Alaska. Should they do this, it would greatly help the statehood cause. So, I went to the 1947 conference, which was held in Salt Lake City.

The Governors' Conferences, at that time, had a three-day program. The Governors would assemble informally on a Sunday and the next three days would be devoted to the official program. On three successive mornings some topic of particular interest would be scheduled, such as education, taxation, highways, tourism. The morning session would be preceded by a breakfast at which approximately one-third of the Governors who were going to take part in that day's discussion would meet and have a sort of dry run of what they were going to discuss. The business session would be continued at lunch time. The afternoons would be devoted to outdoor recreation, golf, tennis, swimming, etc., and there would usually be some entertainment in the evening. The last event of each session— the adoption of resolutions—would take place immediately after luncheon on the third day, Wednesday, after which the Conference would break up.

At that time, the Governors' Conference had adopted a rule that all resolutions had to be passed by unanimous vote. The reason for that was that a controversial issue on which, let us say, the Governors would split perhaps 24 to 18, allowing for a few absentees, would be inconclusive and possibly divisive—hence, the unanimity rule. A Resolutions Committee, consisting of an equal number of Republicans and Democrats, would pass on these resolutions, which, if approved, would come up for action after lunch on Wednesday, the last day, as the final act of the conference.

I had appeared before the Resolutions Committee to ask it to pass a pro-statehood resolution, a draft of which I submitted. There was a little amusement at what, to some of the Eastern and Southern Governors, was a novel idea, and some opposition was voiced.[3] I was told that if a resolution was to be considered for Alaska, there would have to be one also for Hawaii. I wholly favored this. In fact, during the years of my campaigning for statehood, I would constantly reiterate that Hawaii deserved it more but that Alaska needed it more. Hawaii deserved it more because "The Paradise of the Pacific" had the requisite population for more than one member of Congress, approximately half a million people, a going economy, and a revenue system, whereas Alaska's population was far from that required for one member of Congress, we had no adequate tax program, and our economy was still full of uncertainties.

The Governor of Hawaii at that time was Ingram M. Stainback, a former United States District Judge, who was not enthusiastic about statehood, and so it fell upon me to present the case somewhat for both Pacific territories. However, he gave statehood lip service and finally two resolutions, one for Alaska and one for Hawaii, which I drafted, were approved. The Alaska resolution was as follows:

"Alaska"

"The people of Alaska have at the ballot box expressed their de-

sire to achieve statehood. Alaska is one of the two incorporated territories of the United States for which statehood, following American
tradition and precedent, is "clearly indicated as their destiny. Alaska
has been under the American flag for eighty years and has therefore undergone a period of preparation and tutelage for longer than
that of most territories, before they achieved statehood. The expressed
wish of our own fellow-citizens of Alaska is merely for the fulfillment
of the moderate, understandable, traditional and legitimate aspiration
to achieve full equality and responsibility in the family of states and
for self-government according to the established American pattern.

"Therefore, the Governors' Conference hereby expresses its sympathy with the recorded desire for statehood of the people of Alaska,
and endorses the passage of suitable legislation by the Congress to
achieve that end."

I recall gratefully that the Governors who were the most helpful
in support of the statehood resolution were: Sidney P. Osborn, of
Arizona, who told me he remembered the days when Arizona had
suffered, before becoming a state in 1912, all the disadvantages of
a territorial status; Earl Warren, of California; Lee Knous, of Col-
orado; John L. McConaghy, of Connecticut; Charles H. Robins, of
Idaho; Robert Bradford, of Massachusetts; Luther Youngdahl, of
Minnesota; Sam C. Ford, of Montana; Val Peterson, of Nebraska;
Vail Pittman, of Nevada; Alfred E. Driscoll, of New Jersey;
Thomas J. Mabry, of New Mexico; Ray J. Turner, of Oklahoma;
Earl Snell, of Oregon; James H. Duff, of Pennsylvania; John O.
Pastore, of Rhode Island; Ernest Gibson, of Vermont; and Lester C.
Hunt, of Wyoming.

It was a great thrill when the resolution supporting the admission of Alaska was adopted. I knew it would be of much help to
our cause that the Governors of the already existing states, all of
them long in the Union, were voting to include two territories that
were not contiguous to the existing bloc of states.

But there was sufficient discussion and expression of doubt that
I felt that if this favorable result were to be repeated, I would have
to attend all the remaining conferences as long as I was Governor.

In the 1948 conference, which was held in Portsmouth, New
Hampshire, I presented the same resolution as had been adopted by
the 1947 Governors' Conference and expected that this time it
would pass without difficulty. However, a friendly Governor, Roy
Turner, of Oklahoma, came to me and said: "You better get
down to that meeting of the Resolutions Committee." Stainback,
Hawaii's Governor, has been there and told them that Communism
was rampant in Hawaii, and while he did not say he was opposed
to statehood, he left the definite impression that this was not the
time to grant statehood to Hawaii, and if Hawaii is dropped, Alaska
might well be also."

So, I found myself defending the cause of Hawaiian statehood
vigorously. Having worked closely with Samuel Wilder King, Hawaii's Delegate in Congress, a graduate of the Naval Academy
Class of 1910, later Territorial Governor of Hawaii, who re-entered

the Naval Service as a four-striper after Pearl Harbor, and with his successor, Joseph Rider Farrington, editor and publisher of the Honolulu Star-Bulletin, I knew that the tales of Communism in Hawaii were grossly exaggerated and were being propagated by opponents of statehood. So, I managed to get the resolutions for both Territories adopted a second time.

There was no difficulty at the next Governors' Conference at Colorado Springs in 1949. For Oren Long, a strong advocate of statehood, had become Governor, later to be one of Hawaii's first two Senators, and thus these two Pacific territories presented a united front at this and at the next Governors' Conference.

But another difficulty arose at the 1950 conference at White Sulphur Springs, Virginia. It was after lunch on the last day, Wednesday, June 21st. Presiding was Governor Frank Lausche, of Ohio. As he went down the list of resolutions which were invariably approved by a chorus of "ayes" and no "noes", he came to the resolution that Alaska and Hawaii be admitted as States. When he called for any opposed, there was one loud "no". It came from Governor Herman Talmadge, of Georgia.

"The motion is defeated", said presiding officer Lausche. There was a breathless pause at this unexpected development. At this point, Governor Alfred Driscoll, of New Jersey, spoke up. "This resolution has passed three previous Governors' Conferences. Would the distinguished Governor of Georgia tell us why he opposes it?" "I don't mind at all," said Governor Talmadge. "The people I represent are opposed to the admission of any states whose Senators are not likely to take our position on cloture." This was a reference to the preoccupation of the Southern states to be able to indulge in unlimited debate, i.e., to filibuster, in the United States Senate, to prevent civil rights legislation from passing.

I rose and addressed my remarks to Governor Talmadge. I pointed out Alaska's need for statehood. I went into the discriminations which Alaska was enduring as a result of its territorial status. After I talked for about fifteen minutes, I could sense that most of the Governors were getting fidgety. This was the last item on the agenda and the last act of the Conference. All were anxious to get away. After I talked for some time, Governor Frederick Payne, of Maine, who was friendly to our cause, and whom I had gotten to know well because of my newspaper editorship in Portland, Maine, rose, went over to Talmadge, and whispered something in his ear. I continued to speak. Another Governor, Sidney McMath, of Arkansas, followed suit. What they were saying, they told me later, was: "Please lay off, Herman. This guy is going to keep us here all afternoon." They were right. I was determined there would be no cloture on my remarks.

At this point, Governor Talmadge rose and asked me to yield. He said: "I shall withdraw my vote in opposition to statehood; I want the record to show that I am not voting, but that if I did vote, it would be against statehood."

I thanked Governor Talmadge for his gallantry and have never forgotten it. His action made it possible for the statehood resolution to pass.

A similar proceeding took place at my last Governors' Conference in Houston in 1952. There, two other Southern Governors, James Byrnes, of South Carolina, and John S. Battle, of Virginia, likewise opposed to statehood for the same reason Governor Talmadge had been, joined him in announcing their opposition to the resolution but abstaining from voting, so that the resolution would not be defeated. By this time, other Governors who had not been at the earlier conference were ready to support it. Among them were: Elbert Carvel, of Delaware; Len Jordan, of Idaho; Henry F. Schricker, of Indiana; Edward F. Arn, of Kansas; Theodore R. McKeldin, of Maryland; G. Mennen Williams, of Michigan; John W. Bonner, of Montana; W Kerr Scott, of North Carolina; and Arthur Langlie, of Washington.

But it was the last time that a resolution for statehood for Alaska and Hawaii was sought and adopted at the Governors' Conference. I was fearful that the failure of my successors to seek one in the ensuing six years before statehood was adopted would be used as an argument against it. It would be said, I feared, that the Governors of the States had changed their minds. Indeed, it was suggested by a columnist reporting on the 1953 Conference; but by that time, public opinion for statehood had risen beyond recall, and the States' Governors' support was no longer as necessary as it had been, as long as they did not reverse their previous endorsement of statehood.

MEANWHILE; a concurrent and continuing effort had to be made at home, in Alaska, to win public opinion more strongly for statehood. This involved, in essence, a program of adult education, presenting and emphasizing the facts about the benefits that statehood and self-government would bring. These benefits might seem to most Americans to be fully self-evident, but the largely unexpressed aspirations of Alaskans for a larger measure of home rule and self-government were always inhibited by the efforts of the strong mining, fishing and transportation interests, which were almost entirely absentee-owned, and their active resident allies in the form of local agents, members of chamber of commerce executive committees, insurance company representatives and the like. Then, too, Alaska had for so long lived without the blessings of self-government that many of them of longest residence—the old-timers and pioneers—were sincerely opposed because they had either forgotten or had never known at the early ages most of them left the States what a precious and essential tool of liberty the handling of their own governmental affairs in Alaska and voting representation in Congress constituted.

Thus, statehood became inevitably a political issue in Alaska. It became an issue which decided many elections to the Territorial Legislature. Those who had enlisted in the statehood cause had to find likely candidates for office who were favorable to it, had to persuade them to run and generate the publicity and support necessary to gain their election. Probably in a real sense statehood was *the* political issue in Alaska after 1946, separating those who preferred to cling to an old way from those who looked forward to a more active, progressing and more rewarding Alaska in the future.

Of the greatest assistance to the statehood cause was the Alaska Statehood Association, formed largely through the leadership of Robert B. and Evangeline Atwood. It was a voluntary citizens association meeting its expenditures through the dues of its membership and from donations from public-spirited citizens, such as Zachary Loussac, Anchorage Democrat. Starting in Anchorage, it established branches in other Alaskan communities. Its most notable contribution was a study entitled: "Statehood for Alaska: The Issues Involved and the Facts About the Issues", written by George Sundborg. William L. Baker, editor of the *Ketchikan Chronicle,* printed it as a supplement in his newspaper and, because of its news value, several other newspaper editors were persuaded to do likewise, the costs in some instances being borne by the Association. It was then issued as a 56-page pamphlet in July, 1946, and widely distributed. Its foreword stated frankly that "The Association was formed primarily to win the referendum vote but its members, Alaskans from all sections of the Territory, realize that statehood cannot be attained in a day, and even after the U. S. Congress has enacted the enabling legislation, the State has been set up and its officers have begun to function, the original aims and desires of the people still will have to be sought out and carried forward."

The 1949 Legislature was to prove the greatest and most productive in the history of the Territory. Besides enacting the comprehensive revenue measures previously referred to and repairing the damage wrought by the previous 1947 Legislature, it was responsive to the analysis in my message to it of the discriminations which Alaska was suffering that statehood would eliminate, and responded to my plea for affirmative action to hasten its coming.

It created a statehood committee and supplied it with funds— $80,000. It was Senate Bill †49, given its number as a symbol of hope that Alaska would become the 49th State!

It was introduced by Senator Victor Rivers, of Anchorage, and Senator Frank Peratrovich, of Klawock.

It passed the Senate by a vote of 15 to 1.

Those voting for it were: Edward Anderson, Democrat of Nome; Frank Barr, Democrat of Fairbanks; John Butrovich, Jr., Republican of Fairbanks; Earnest B. Collins, Republican of Fairbanks; L. P. Dawes, Republican of Juneau; Gunnard Engebreth, Republican of Anchorage; Anita Garnick, Republican of Juneau; Walter E. Huntley, Democrat of Palmer; Charles D. Jones, Republican of Nome; Howard Lyng, Democrat of Nome; Roderick M. MacKenzie, Democrat of Ketchikan; Steve McCutcheon, Democrat of Anchorage; Andrew Nerland, Republican of Fairbanks; Frank Peratrovich, Democrat of Klawock; Victor C. Rivers, Democrat of Anchorage.

The lone opponent was William Munz, Republican of Nome.

In the House, the vote was 21 to 2, with one absent.

Those supporting it were: G. E. Almquist, Democrat, of Juneau; Abel Anderson, Democrat, of Juneau; Frank Angerman, Democrat, of Fairbanks; Doris Barnes, Republican of Wrangell; William E. Beltz, Democrat, of Nome; C. Chester Carlson, Democrat, of Cordova; Jack D. Conright, Democrat, of Anchorage; Essie Dale, Democrat, of Fairbanks; William A. Egan, Democrat, of Valdez; Glen D. Franklin, Democrat, of Fairbanks; Amelia Gunderson, Democrat, of Ketchikan; Andrew Hope, Democrat, of Sitka; Percy Ipalook, Republican, of Wales; Frank G. Johnson, Republican, of Kake; Frank L. Johnson, Democrat, of Nome; Clarence P. Keating, Democrat of Seward; Stanley J. McCutcheon, Democrat, of Anchorage; James Nolan, Democrat, of Wrangell; Alfred A. Owen, Jr., Democrat, of Anchorage; Clayton A. Pollard, Democrat, of Kasilof; and Warren A. Taylor, Democrat, of Fairbanks.

Opposed were: George J. Miscovich, Republican, of Fairbanks; Almer Rydeen, Democrat of Nome.

Absent: Marcus F. Jensen, Democrat, of Douglas.

I signed the bill on March 25th.

The Act provided that the Statehood Committee should consist of eleven members appointed by the Governor, and that not more than six should be members of the same party. The nominees were to be confirmed or rejected by a majority of the members of both houses assembled in joint session.

Selecting this important committee presented some problems—problems which perhaps every State executive has experienced, although they were rather special in this case.

At that time, Alaska had four judicial divisions, which were likewise the legislative divisions, whose people had a definite sense of local consciousness and desire for recognition of this area. In other words, I should have at least two committee members from each of the four divisions.

It was necessary, I felt, also to recognize the racial aspects. It seemed clearly desirable to me that at least one representative of the Indian and one of the Eskimo people be appointed. Certainly at least one woman should be on the committee.

So, from the First Division, southeastern Alaska, I nominated William L. Baker, Democrat, then the editor and publisher of the Ketchikan Chronicle, and Mildred R. Hermann, Republican, former President of the State Federation of Women's Clubs, an attorney, and a public-spirited citizen from Juneau.

From the Second Division, along the Arctic and Bering Sea, I nominated Howard Lyng, Democrat, miner, Democratic National Committeeman, and Percy Ipalook, Republican, both members of the legislature.

From the Third Division, I proposed Robert B. Atwood, Republican, editor and publisher of the Anchorage Times; Stanley J. McCutcheon, Democrat, attorney, Speaker of the House; Victor Rivers, Democrat, civil engineer and Territorial Senator; and Lee Bettinger, Republican, businessman, Mayor of Kodiak.

From the Fourth Division, I nominated Andrew Nerland, of Fairbanks, Republican, merchant, who had served longer in the legislatures than anyone, and was President of the Board of Regents of the University of Alaska; and Warren A. Taylor, of Fairbanks, Democrat, attorney and legislator who had represented three different areas in the legislature, namely, Cordova and Kodiak, previous to his election from Fairbanks.

So, to start with, every one of the four divisions was represented by at least one Republican and one Democrat. The ethnic diversity I sought to recognize by nominating Frank Peratrovich, Democrat, of Klawock, the outstanding representative of Alaska's Indian people, who had been in the legislature since 1945, was destined to be the first Vice President of the Constitutional Convention and President of both the Territorial and State Senate; and Percy Ipalook, Presbyterian Minister and the first Eskimo to serve in the legislature. I therefore felt quite pleased in feeling that I had met all the different requirements that seemed to me essential within the limitation of having to divide the committee 6 to 5 between our two political parties. However, when these nominees came before the joint session for confirmation, my selection was severely criticized by John Butrovich, Senator from Fairbanks, one of the ablest and most enlightened of our legislators, who stated that he could recognize as a good Republican among the six selected only Andrew Nerland. Why he thus disqualified Bob Atwood, Mildred Hermann, Percy Ipalook and Lee Bettinger was a mystery to me then and thereafter, and I was distressed at his criticism because of my high regard for him and his judgment. However, the nominations were all confirmed.

Bob Atwood was elected Chairman, Bill Baker Vice-Chairman of the Committee, Mildred Hermann Secretary, and Delegate Bob Bartlett and his predecessor as delegate, Judge Anthony J. Dimond, and I were named ex officio members.

This Committee proved to be invaluable and carried on an intensive publicity campaign which helped tremendously to promote our statehood cause. Among its many activities were to stimulate letters from Alaskans to their relatives and friends in the States, asking them to write their Senators and Representatives urging support for statehood legislation.

I T now seemed to me that we ought to get up a national committee of distinguished Americans who would support the statehood cause, and I began a campaign of letter writing and personal contact in order to secure a committee of one hundred. I completed its formation in 1949, and it consisted of the following:

Ellis Arnall
Gen. H. H. Arnold
Rex Beach
Dave Beck
Adolf A. Berle, Jr.
Francis Biddle
Sarah Gibson Blanding
Harold Boeschenstein
Gov. John W. Bonner
Joe E. Brown
Belmore Browne
Mrs. J. L. Blair Buck
Pearl S. Buck
Rear Adm. Richard E. Byrd
James Cagney
Ward Canaday
Arthur Capper
William S. Carlson
Hodding Carter
Stuart Chase
Morris Llewellyn Cooke
Bartley Crum
Homer Cummings
Jonathan Daniels
Jay N. Darling
Clarence R. Decker
John Dewey
Maj. Gen. Wm. J. Donovan
Michael Francis Doyle
Gov. Alfred E. Driscoll
Cyrus Eaton, Jr.
Maj. George Fielding Eliot
James A. Farley
Marshall Field III
Dorothy Canfield Fisher
Douglas Southall Freeman
Ira N. Gabrielson
John Nance Garner

William Green
Joseph C. Grew
John Gunther
Vice Adm. Harry Hamlet
Mrs. J. Borden Harriman
Oveta Culp Hobby
Hamilton Holt
Palmer Hoyt
Rupert Hughes
Croil Hunter
Mrs. Ellsworth Huntington
Eric Johnston
Al Jolson
Jesse Holman Jones
Bishop Gerald K. Kennedy
Robert M. La Follette, Jr.
James M. Landis
Wilbur LaRoe, Jr.
Herbert H. Lehman
Gov. Thomas J. Mabry
Gen. Douglas MacArthur
Archibald MacLeish
E. B. MacNaughton
Gov. Sidney S. McMath
Malcolm Muir
Philip Murray
Jeannette Paddock Nichols
Reinhold Niebuhr
Adm. Chester W. Nimitz
Howard W. Odum
Robert P. Patterson
Gov. Val Peterson
Cornelia Bryce Pinchot
Daniel A. Poling
Henry Varnum Poor
Grantland Rice
Eddie Rickenbacker
Kenneth Roberts

Eleanor Roosevelt
James Roosevelt
Arthur Schlesinger, Jr.
Robert E. Sherwood
Kenneth C. M. Sills
James G. Stahlman
Vilhjalmur Stefansson
Gov. Adlai E. Stevenson
John W. Studebaker
Herbert Bayard Swope

Gov. Roy J. Turner
Gov. Earl Warren
Bradford Washburn
Wallace H. White, Jr.
Gov. G. Mennen Williams
Joseph R. Wilson
Henry M. Wriston
Wilson W. Wyatt
Alvin C. York
Darryl F. Zanuck

I wonder, eighteen years later, how many of our fellow-Alaskans can identify these individuals. All were outstanding in the fields of government, military service, literature, the arts, business, and in many other respects.

Their support carried substantial weight in many quarters. Having the five-star Generals of the Air Force (Arnold) and of the Army (MacArthur), and a five-star Admiral (Nimitz), the Secretary of War (Patterson), Rear Admiral Richard E. Byrd, and "Wild Bill" Donovan, wartime head of the O. S. S., as well as George Fielding Eliot, noted writer on military topics, among our supporters, played its part in getting military approval of statehood. Having three prominent Texans—Jesse Jones, John Nance Garner, and Oveta Culp Hobby, would bring us at least one Texan Representative's vote in the final statehood action. Eleanor Roosevelt, to whom I had presented the case for statehood, thereafter spoke for it and wrote about it in her daily newspaper column. Others of these national committee members pitched in actively to persuade their Senators and Representatives to support statehood.

Hearings on statehood bills began in the 80th Congress on April 16, 1947, in the House of Representatives. Under consideration was H. R. 206, introduced by Delegate E. L. (Bob) Bartlett. Presiding at the hearing was Representative Fred Crawford, of Michigan, Chairman of the Subcommittee on Territorial and Insular Possessions of the Committee on Public Lands. It is interesting, twenty years later, to recall the roster of witnesses, pro and con.

Secretary of the Interior Julius A. Krug, the first witness, strongly supported the legislation and was questioned at length by the committee members.

He was followed by Rep. Henry D. Larcade, Jr., Democrat, of Louisiana, likewise a warm supporter of statehood, a rare occurrence among representatives from the South, especially the deep South.

Anthony J. Dimond, Alaska's former delegate, then a Federal District Judge in Anchorage, who had sponsored statehood legislation while in Congress, spoke with effective earnestness.

Following him came the favorable testimony of Rep. Homer D. Angell, Republican, of Oregon. He introduced into the record a supporting letter from Arthur J. Farmer, General Manager of the Portland Chamber of Commerce, the first chamber on the Pacific

Coast to endorse Alaskan statehood. That concluded the first day's hearing.

The second day, April 17th, began with a fine supporting statement by Representative Mike Mansfield, of Montana, later destined to be the Majority Leader of the Senate. He was followed by Representative George P. Miller, Democrat, of California, then serving his second term, and now, twenty years later, the second ranking member of the 38-member California delegation in the House.

Marion T. Bennett, Republican, of Missouri, followed. He had been in Alaska in 1945 as a member of the House Subcommittee on Territories, and I had accompanied it around Alaska and had had a good chance to indoctrinate him.

Representative Harold C. Hagen, Republican, of Minnesota, followed with a favorable statement. A brother of his was a resident of the Matanuska Valley.

The first adverse witness followed. He was Herbert L. Faulkner, Republican, a Juneau attorney, whose law firm, which he headed, represented the large absentee interests.

On the third day, April 18th, witnesses favorable to statehood were Hugh Dougherty, of Anchorage, insurance agent, representing the Anchorage Chamber of Commerce; Representative Melvin Price, Democrat, of Illinois, still in Congress, and in 1967 second ranking in the 24-member Illinois House delegation. He was followed by Rep. Melvin Snyder, Republican, an attorney of West Virginia, who had served in the Army in Alaska during World War II, continuing there as Territorial Surplus Property Officer for the Department of the Interior. He was familiar at first hand with Alaska, and it was his view that statehood was desirable because it would lessen "the hold of the Interior Department", which he testified "has strangled in many ways the development of the Territory." (That, in my view, has been true both before and since statehood.)

Harrie O. Bohlke, Director of Industrial Relations of the Seattle Industrial Commission, listed the discriminations Alaska had suffered as a result of the territorial status and alluded to the exploitation of Alaska by Seattle residents.

William L. Baker, editor and publisher of the Ketchikan Chronicle, testified at length, making a strong case for statehood.

The next witness was Richard F. Lewis, a resident of San Francisco, owner of the water system of Juneau. He felt that the people of Alaska could not afford the costs of statehood. Subsequent witnesses castigated him as a typical absentee owner.

Following him, witnesses favorable to statehood were: Ken Hinchey, building contractor of Anchorage; Lee Bettinger, Mayor of Kodiak; Rep. Albert Gore, Democrat, of Tennessee; George Sundborg, General Manager of the Alaska Development Board, who presented a thorough analysis of the economic facts that would justify statehood, and Ralph J. Rivers, Attorney General of Alaska.

Jack McCord, of McCord, Alaska, a stockman who had lived in Alaska over forty years, testified that he was "against statehood at this time. The principal reason," he stated, was that Alaska had "only about 80,000 permanent population," which was not sufficient to take care of the extra expenditures statehood would require.

C. M. Granger, of the National Forest Service, took no position on statehood, but raised and answered some questions about the national forests in Alaska, and Charles E. Kellogg, of the Division of Soil Surveys of the Department of Agriculture, stressed the importance of soil surveys by the Federal Government to assist the State in its beginnings.

Emil Hurja, who had gone to Alaska and engaged in journalism as a young man, and was associated with Charles A. Sulzer, Alaska's Delegate to the 65th Congress, testified that "statehood for Alaska is long overdue."

Fred Mallery Packard, of the National Parks Association, testified against the provision in H. R. 206 that would turn over the Katmai, Sitka and Kasaan National Monuments to the State while retaining Mt. McKinley National Park and Glacier Bay National Monument under Federal control. (All except Kasaan, which was abandoned, were, in subsequent statehood legislation, retained by the Federal Government.) Bob Bartlett took advantage of Packard's appearance to bring out the lack of visitors' accommodations in Glacier Bay and Katmai, which Packard explained was due to lack of funds.

Robert B. Atwood, Editor and Publisher of the Anchorage Times, Alaska's newspaper of widest circulation, testified on the forces opposing statehood. Said he: "Mr. Faulkner and Mr. Lewis are the voices of the same groups and influences that have opposed every progressive measure that has been enacted in the past to build up the government of Alaska."

Atwood had done considerable research, and in response to questioning by Bob Bartlett, produced pertinent statistical tables that were inserted in the record of the hearing.

Welch Pogue, a practicing attorney of Washington, D. C., President of the National Aeronautics Association and former Chairman of the Civil Aeronautics Board, testified in favor of statehood, both for himself and his client, Alaska Airlines. He gave his view that Alaska was "the only Gibraltar of the air age. No other body of land . . . is as necessary to get from one continent to the other in the air."

Chat Paterson, Legislative Representative of the American Veterans Committee (Amvets) testified of the desire of World War II veterans to settle in Alaska, and expressed the feeling of his organization that statehood would make this objective more attainable.

Steve Larrson Homer, President of the Veterans Alaska Cooperative Co., which had recently secured Chilkoat Barracks, testified similarly as to the desirability of getting World War II veterans to Alaska and how those who had exercised and prized the right to vote for President and for a voting delegation in Congress would feel deprived without it if Alaska remained a territory.

Don Carlos Brownell, Territorial Senator, who had come to Alaska with his parents in 1899, had settled in Seward at its beginnings in 1903, had been elected its Mayor nine times and to the Senate four successive times, testified that every effort to develop the Kenai Peninsula since 1903 had been fought by every single (Federal) bureau. The Federal bureaus and the absentee interests, he felt, prevented Alaska's development, and statehood was Alaska's only salvation.

Byron E. Cowart, a retired Army Major who had served as an aide to Lt. Gen. Simon Bolivar Buchner, Jr., as Secretary to the General Staff, as the Alaska Command's Transportation Officer, and later, in the Pentagon, as General Staff Officer in the Alaska section of the Operations Division, advanced a number of arguments for statehood from the military standpoint. He said he expected to make Alaska his home.

My testimony, which required two and a half hours (it occupied 38 pages in the printed record), concluded the hearings. They had lasted seven days. I had listened to all the testimony, and Bob Bartlett, who was invariably the final interrogator of each witness, effectively elaborated on the aspects brought out by each.

The Subcommittee had been most kind and generous throughout. Preston E. Peden, Democrat, of Oklahoma, said at the conclusion of my testimony:

> "Governor, I think there is one thing that the record fails to show and that is the deep sincerity with which you made the statement before this committee. It is my belief that if all members of Congress would have heard you and Mr. Sundborg, there would be little doubt as to the outcome of this plea for statehood."

And the Subcommittee voted to report the bill unanimously to the full Committee, which in turn reported it unanimously. Its Chairman was Richard J. Welch, Republican, of California.[1]

It is saddening to think that today not a single one of these Representatives remains in Congress, but their names deserve recording: Republicans—Fred L. Crawford, Michigan; Karl M. Le-Compte, Iowa; William Lemke, North Dakota; Dean P. Taylor, New York; Jay LeFevre, New York; A. L. Miller, Nebraska; Norris Poulsen, California; Charles H. Russell, Nevada; John Sanborn, Idaho; Edward H. Jenison, Illinois; William A. Dawson, Utah. Democrats—C. Jasper Bell, Missouri; Antonio M. Fernandez, New Mexico; Clair Engle, California; E. H. Hedrick, West Virginia; Preston E. Peden, Oklahoma; Monroe M. Redden, North Carolina.

Further hearings took place in Alaska that Summer of 1947 by four members of the subcommittee consisting of Fred L. Crawford, as Chairman; Jay LeFevre; William A. Dawson; and Edward H. Jenison. The committee heard witnesses in Anchorage, Seward, Fairbanks, Barrow, Nome, Kodiak, Cordova, Juneau, Petersburg, Wrangell and Ketchikan, and went into the great variety of problems that confronted the people in these diverse communities. Bob Bartlett, of course, accompanied the committee, as did George Sundborg, my Executive Assistant and consultant to the Alaska

Development Board. I attended the hearings in Juneau and Ketchikan, as well as some hearings by a subcommittee of the Senate
Public Lands Committee, which I accompanied throughout Alaska,
consisting of Hugh Butler, R. of Nebraska, as Chairman; Ernest
McFarland, D. of Arizona; and Zales Ecton, R. of Montana. I had
to divide my time between these committees as well as another
Senate committee consisting of Allen Ellender, D., of Louisiana;
Homer Capehart, R., of Indiana; and Harry Cain, R., of Washington, who were investigating Alaska's timber resources in relation
to pending legislation which would facilitate the establishment of
pulp mills. Statehood and Alaska's other numerous problems were
to get a thorough airing.

At Anchorage on August 30th, the first of the House committee
hearings, Mayor Francis C. Bowden, strongly urging statehood,
illustrated one of Alaska's problems by citing the difficulty Anchorage had had in getting legislation to permit it to bond itself for
needed municipal improvements.

"The legislation", he testified, "was bottled up in Congress
for a long time. Our delegate. . . . after diligent inquiry, learned
that one member objected on the grounds that $8,000,000 was too
much. . . . for Anchorage to spend. Need of the projects had nothing to do with it. The plight of Anchorage was unknown to this
Congressman. He had never been here. He was totally ignorant of
the facts concerned. A compromise was necessary. This Congressman offered to withdraw his objection provided one item. . . .
$100,000 for an athletic field was eliminated and the total au-
thorization reduced to $5,000,000." So, "Anchorage, due to the
whim of a Congressman who is not concerned nor informed, was
deprived of carrying forward a program of most essential public
utilities."

"Alaskans generally and especially the people of Anchorage",
Mayor Bowden concluded, "do not like their present status as
eunuchs among the citizens of the United States."

Mrs. Robert S. Lippencott, testifying from the standpoint of a
homesteader, pointed to Alaska's roadlessness as an obstacle to
homesteading.

State Senator Victor Rivers, chairman of the Senate Taxation
Committee, detailed the activities by the absentee interests in
blocking revenue legislation and keeping themselves untaxed.

Mrs. Josefina Seiler, wife of a C. A. A. official and pilot, won-
dered "how on earth are we going to teach our children here in
Alaska democracy when under the present form of government
we are so far from the democratic ideal?"

Dorothy Tyner, attorney, urged that all that Alaska was asking
for was "a chance to solve its own problems."

Evangeline Atwood (Mrs. Robert B. Atwood), born and reared
in Alaska, trained social case worker, who in 1945 had organized
the Alaska Statehood Association to study the issues involved in
changing from a Territory to a State status, in preparation for
the referendum on statehood for the Fall of 1946, detailed several

"instances of the thwarting of Alaska's potential development" by distant Federal agencies.

"Having someone 6,000 miles away tell us how to run our affairs is mighty bitter medicine," she said.

At the second day's hearing, Edwin M. Suddock, merchandiser, testified at length on the history and contemporary condition of water transportation. He outlined the absorption of one steamship company after another until all maritime transportation was controlled by the Alaska Steamship Company of Seattle, of whose performance he was highly critical. "It writes the ticket for most of Alaska. . . . all of the things that the Alaska Steamship Company has contributed to Alaska in the way of permanent assets could be put on a wheelbarrow. . . . we believe that one of the primary reasons for being a State in Alaska is to get our hand in this thing . . . and see if we can't make some changes."

"We believe Alaskans should have some say. . . .".

"Nothing. . . . has prevented Alaska's growth as much as this lack of economical transportation."

Del Van Curler, chairman of the Committee of Alaska Railroad Labor Organizations, representing 2,000 employees, declared his support for statehood for eight reasons, the first being "that during 80 years of bureaucratic control Alaska's natural resources have not been normally developed."

Elmer Rasmuson, banker, contrasted the expenditures made by the Federal Government to promote democracy in foreign lands with its "close regard for the financial side" in American Territories. Statehood, he felt, would increase the flow of private capital to Alaska.

Major Marvin R. Marston, who had spent 5 1/2 years in military service in Alaska and had organized the Eskimo units of the Alaska Territorial Guard, said: "In the 80 years we have governed Alaska by ignorance, neglect and exploitation. . ." and "let's make the moose move over and do let us have this (state) to run."

Raymond Marshall, Chairman of the Board of Alaska Airlines, the private enterprise with the Territory's largest payroll, testified that while its capital came from the States, it had come to develop the Territory and not like other absentee interests to take something out.

J. L. McCarrey, attorney, appeared for himself and the Anchorage Chamber of Commerce, in which, he testified, there was not one dissenting vote on statehood.

Other witnesses for statehood were: John Hedberg, known as "Moosemeat John"; Rev. R. Rolland Armstrong, Presbyterian minister; John Manders, attorney and former Mayor of Anchorage; and John F Gorsuch, who presented a statement from the American Legion, Department of Alaska, favoring statehood.

Lee Gardner gave a detailed and vivid account of arbitrary actions by Federal bureaus adversely affecting Alaskans, which he felt would not be cured by statehood.

Steve McCutcheon, in an impassioned plea, concluded with

the request: "Make us full partners in the Union of the States, or by God, make us a free nation."

At Fairbanks on September 3rd:

Art Glover, minerologist for the Territorial Department of Mines, analyzed the high living costs in Alaska but was doubtful whether statehood would reduce them.

Norman Stines, mining engineer, representing, he said, the majorities in the second and fourth divisions who had voted against statehood, listed all the advantages cited by proponents of statehood and then offered a refutation of each. He was sharply cross-questioned by Delegate Bartlett.

Al Anderson, Executive Secretary of the Alaska Miners Association, felt that the referendum on statehood showed that Alaskans were "certainly not zealous for statehood." Also, "the talk of Alaska's great resources. . . . are grossly exaggerated, so that the sources of revenue to run the new State are limited indeed."

Mrs. Alaska Stewart Linck, former Territorial legislator, opposed statehood because its area was too big and not contiguous to the United States, its population too small, with too few White people, and statehood would bring "additional burdens" and "new expenses".

Luther C. Hess, attorney with mining interests, and former Territorial legislator, was opposed to statehood "at this time".

Clarence Moriarty, representing a stateside construction company, declared that "statehood for Alaska at this time is little short of suicide."

Mrs. Margaret Smith, paying a warm tribute to the character and capabilities of Alaskans, felt that they could make a success of statehood. Countering previous witnesses' reflections, she rejected their assertions that "the native population should be considered a dead weight on our economy. . . . . We have too many examples of outstanding contributions by those of native blood to question that the potentialities are within them to help in the task of building a State."

Paul Huebner testified that the Territory's Organic Act was "an oxen's yoke around our necks" and that "we desire voting representation in Washington, D. C.".

Andrew Nerland, born in Norway, who had served in ten legislative sessions and was then President of the Senate, said he had come to Seattle three months after Washington had become a State and was impressed with what statehood had done for it.

John E. Pegues, newspaperman, who had lived in Alaska 38 years, said he had "advocated statehood for many years".

Cecil Wells, automotive distributor and gold miner, said he dissented from the mining industry's opposition to statehood.

Maurice T. Johnson, lawyer and Territorial legislator, felt that while "statehood is a laudable ambition", he was "certain . . . that we are not anywhere near ready for statehood from the standpoint of practical economics."

Mr. W. C. Arnold, managing director of the Alaska Salmon Industry, Inc., and its effective lobbyist at the sessions of the Territorial Legislature, who generally followed Congressional committees coming to Alaska, testified three times—at Fairbanks on September 4th, at Juneau on September 9th, and at Ketchikan on September 12th. In these hearings he voiced no opposition to statehood, felt that discussion of it was not untimely—indeed, he did not advocate delaying it—but believed that Alaska's critical problems should first be disposed of. He thought that Alaska could not develop "until some stable transportation system is effected where goods can move into and out of this Territory on a stable basis at a reasonable rate" and that "the approach ought to be about putting our house in order by solving the problems which confront us and which would enable us to develop the Territory and statehood to come as a natural development."

However, a few weeks earlier, at Anchorage, before Senator Butler's subcommittee, Mr. Arnold stated flatly:

"The Alaska Salmon Industry is opposed to statehood. We're paying most of the cost of running the Territory now. We don't propose to pick up the check for the additional cost of statehood." (The Butler subcommittee hearings were not reported but I was present and noted Mr. Arnold's testimony.)

Irving Reed, mining engineer, declared: "We had more hopes for Alaska back in 1915 than now, and we don't seem to be getting any place without it (statehood)."

Frank Angerman, representing Labor, testified that the working people of Alaska wanted statehood.

Georg Nelson Meyers felt that people of the 48 states should become less ignorant about Alaska and that Alaskans should prepare themselves better for statehood.

Harry Palmer, representing the Fairbanks Junior Chamber of Commerce, which had endorsed statehood at its Departmental Convention, as had the National Jaycees, urged that the national policy of favoring self-determination for other countries should apply to Alaska.

Earl Haussman, owner of the Fairbanks Piggly-Wiggly store, favored statehood, saying:

"Most of the witnesses against statehood have said we can't afford statehood. They have said we don't even raise by taxes the amount needed to support decent Territorial government. Gentlemen, they ought to know because almost without exception the very people who have appeared on this stage to oppose statehood for Alaska have been those who have busied themselves at Juneau during sessions of our Territorial legislature to see that all progressive tax legislation was defeated and the will of the people of Alaska for good government was overthrown, just as they now attempt to overthrow the clearly expressed will of the people of Alaska in the matter of statehood."

At Juneau, on September 8th, Allen Shattuck, insurance man and Territorial legislator, opposed statehood because of the high costs it would impose.

Robert Sheldon, Director of the Territorial Unemployment Compensation Commission, began his testimony by saying:

"I feel, after 50 years continuous residence in Alaska, that if Alaska isn't ready now for statehood it never will be, because the same special interests that have controlled to a great extent the economic history of Alaska for the past 50 years would probably see that no development would take place that would change the status of Alaska in the next 10 years, as in the past 40. I say 10 years because it would probably take 10 years to get statehood working in Alaska if it was authorized tomorrow."

Mrs. Mildred Hermann offered refutation of the statehood costs and revenue figures of Shattuck and Faulkner and introduced a brief by George W. Rogers, an economist, presenting a different outlook.

Delegate Bartlett asked Mrs. Hermann the following question:

"The allegation has been made . . . that the majority of Alaskans voted for statehood because they were high-pressured into it. It was alleged that they were gripped by emotion, excitement, and almost hysteria on account of strikes . . . and that if a calmer atmosphere had prevailed, they would have not voted for statehood in such numbers. What is your opinion as to that?"

Mrs. Hermann replied:

"Well, I think that is pretty much bushwa . . . A whole lot of high pressuring was done to make them think it was going to cost them too much but not at all to make them see the advantages. The case for statehood was clearly and plainly presented and I don't think that the emotional strain which this particular witness mentioned had anything whatever to do with it. All people come out fighting for something that is vital and as big as statehood and very naturally that is the emotion that was back of the vote and . . . that is the kind of emotion that led us to declare our independence of Great Britain in 1776."

Dr. Earl Albrecht, Commissioner of Health for the Territory, testifying that the death rate from tuberculosis among the native population was sixteen times that in the States, pointed out that the United States Senate, in the last 36 hours of the last session, had denied the Alaska Native Service the funds to maintain the 38 native patients in the Seward Sanitarium, a Federal responsibility. Dr. Albrecht amplified his statement with charts and memoranda illustrating the neglect of the natives' health and consequent excessive mortality as a result of Federal neglect.

At Petersburg on September 10th, Earl Ohmer, known as "the Shrimp King", conducted the hearing which was largely devoted to fishery and transportation problems. On the latter, Earl Ohmer declared:

"I don't believe there is any place in the world for the similar length of haul there is so high a freight rate on general commodities as there is from Seattle to Alaska and return."

In Wrangell, on September 11th: James Nolan and Fred Hanford, local businessmen and Territorial legislators, testified in favor of statehood, as did C. T. Eslick, shingle mill operator, who stressed the discriminatory effect of Section 27 of the Jones Act.

C. Howard Baltzo, President of the Wrangell Chamber of Commerce, whose life career had been in fisheries, and who had been working for the Fish and Wildlife Service in various capacities, spoke on the drastic decline of the salmon; being the principal support of the economy of Southeastern Alaska, that was "now approaching a critical state" and was "almost on the verge of disaster", and then commented perceptively:

"A lot of trouble is caused by people who make important decisions who aren't here. The people who make the most money and make the profits do not live in Alaska. They live in Seattle; they live there; their interests are there. The fishermen never make enough money that they can get out of here. These fishermen do not have the kind of money that enables them to journey to Washington, D.C. and employ lobbyists who can present their case. The problem is plenty now, but it will be a lot more unless they are considered. The ability of the new State of Alaska to finance the fisheries is of first rate importance."

At Ketchikan on September 12 detailed pro-statehood presentations were made by Maurice Oaksmith; William L. Baker, editor and publisher of the Ketchikan Chronicle; Wilfred C. Stump, attorney; L. A. Daniels, President of Ketchikan's Central Labor Council; William K. Boardman, representing the Ketchikan Chamber of Commerce; Norman R. Wulker, druggist and Territorial Senator; Andrew Gunderson, fisherman, representing Igloo No. 16 of the Pioneers of Alaska, who said substantially all the membership—of between 1,300 and 1,400—favored statehood; Robert L. Jernberg, attorney; Joe F. Krause, fisherman and authorized to represent the Ketchikan post of the Veterans of Foreign Wars.

Emory F. Tobin, editor and publisher of the *Alaska Sportsman*, felt that statehood would be unwise at this time.

George Sundborg, testifying at length, summarized his conclusions pertinently as follows:

"Your Committee has been traveling now for two full weeks in Alaska. You have been working diligently to understand our problems and to seek solutions for them. Every place you have visited you have become aware of new problems, and if you traveled a month, or if you traveled a year, or if you traveled perpetually in Alaska, you would encounter new and unsolved problems in every place you went.

"I think you must have it in your minds to ask why Alaska is so beset with diffitulties.

"Why do we have so many problems and how are these problems to be solved? I think the answers are obvious. We are beset by problems because we do not have the means to deal with them ourselves, and because we do not have the political power to obtain solutions from Washington. Our problems will be solved just exactly the way problems have been solved everywhere else under the American flag; namely, by the people themselves under statehood. No other solution would be effective and no other solution would be permanent."

I was asked to make the concluding presentation for what had been an investigation of all of Alaska's problems of unprecedented thoroughness by one of the most conscientious and dedicated Congressional committees in my experience—then and thereafter. My statement, made eleven years before an Alaska statehood bill was finally enacted by the Congress, reflects the problems that beset

Alaska as statehood was for the first time receiving the serious attention of the Congress. I said as follows:

"Mr. Chairman and members of the committee, it is a privilege to be before you. I have testified before your committee in Washington last spring. However, a number of things have happened since that time; the committee has heard much testimony; and there are some aspects of this testimony which I would like to comment upon, trying at the same time to avoid needless duplication.

Let me first say that the House Committee on Territories has, in my judgment, given the finest example that it has ever been my good fortune to witness of an effective study by a congressional committee.

During the nearly 8 years that I have been Governor of Alaska, I have seen many congressional committees, committees both of the Senate and the House, come to Alaska. I think I can state unqualifiedly my view that never has a committee among them worked harder, more faithfully, and more earnestly to get to the bottom of our problems and to secure the information which would enable it to help us help ourselves than has this committee—the Subcommittee on Territories and Insular Possessions of the House Committee on Public Lands.

I may also say that the corresponding committee of the Senate, the Senate Public Lands Committee, three of whose members, under the chairmanship of Senator Butler, have likewise just concluded a visit to the Territory, has shown an equal zeal and interest, and has likewise done nothing but to work hard.

My reason for thus taking the liberty, and possibly the presumption, of rendering this tribute to your committee and its corresponding Senate committee is threefold:

First, I think it only fair that this merited expression of appreciation and praise be made a part of the official record. For we are all aware that Congress comes in for much criticism, some of it uninformed and unjustified, and particularly relating to trips which Congressmen make for purposes of investigation. I therefore think it proper and useful that the public should know, and that it be permanently recorded, that your trip, in the reasoned opinion of those in a position to observe at first-hand, has not been any vacation or any junket, using that last word in the generally accepted journalistic sense, and that you, Chairman Crawford, Mr. LeFevre, Mr. Dawson, and Mr. Jenison, have utilized every moment of your time for work and little or none for recreation, which it would have been a privilege for us to help you secure. Both you and the Senate Public Lands Committee have visited the smaller Alaskan communities, such as Cordova, Kodiak, Wrangell, and Petersburg —the Senate committee likewise including Skagway and Haines, which seldom, if ever, have been honored by a visit of a congressional committee. To make these stops and hold hearings there you had to extend yourselves and to work early and late. I want to express to you my personal appreciation and what I feel confident would likewise be the appreciation of the people of Alaska.

My second reason for wishing thus to comment on the performance of your committee and of the corresponding committee in the
Senate relates to a feeling that I have, a deep-seated feeling, that
the most important task that confronts all us Americans, particularly those of us who are public servants, whether elected or appointed, and this applies also to all other persons not in office who
enjoy the inestimable blessing of American citizenship, is to make
democracy work. We have just fought a second great World War
for the purpose of preserving our democratic way of life. The American people have made great sacrifices in blood and treasure to
demonstrate their faith in and their adherence to the democratic
system. But it should ever be borne in mind that it is as essential
to fight and work for democracy in time of peace as in time of war.
Our democracy can be weakened in time of peace by indifference,
by indolence, by selfishness, by corruption, and by a relaxation of
the eternal vigilance which one of our forefathers rightly pro-
claimed, in imperishable words, was the price of liberty.

Now when a committee of the Congress comes to Alaska and
exhibits as sterling a performance as yours, gives so fine an example of public service as you have, it strengthens the faith of the
people in our democratic form of government, and by the same
token, strengthens the whole democratic system. We know, I regret
to say and I do not hesitate to say so frankly, that other congressional committees have come to Alaska whose exhibition has been
different and whose performance correspondingly has caused skep-
ticism and cynicism about our government and our democracy and
to that extent has weakened the faith of some of our citizens and
thereby impaired and injured the democratic process. So I feel
that you have made a great contribution—an over-all contribution—
in addition to what you have accomplished specifically in the particular mission which brought you to Alaska—namely to study the
question of statehood and the other related Alaskan matters.

My third reason for stressing your fine and earnest performance
is that having thus, as one might say, reached a crescendo, I now
regretfully begin a diminuendo by telling you I do not think that this
committee will be able to accomplish the things that it hopes to do
for Alaska except in one way. I will anticipate my conclusion by
saying that one way, and the only way, is to give us statehood.

Year after year, congressional committees and other Government officials in the executive branches have come to Alaska to
study our problems. While, as I have indicated, not all have been
equally zealous and equally indefatigable, over all and collectively,
they have sought to learn what our problems were and are, have
aroused high hopes and gone back with varying degrees of determination to bring about certain reforms legislatively or otherwise that they were convinced were clearly needed. But over the
years very little has happened. The same problems have remained
unsolved; and so my third purpose then is to emphasize especially
my regretful belief that this committee, which has become so keenly aware of many of our problems, has formed its opinions that
certain measures, reforms, and other actions legislatively or ad-

ministratively are needed, and is obviously desirous of doing something about them, will not succeed in achieving such objectives to any material degree. That is not due, clearly, to any failure or shortcoming on your part, either in the immediate past while you were making your study, in the immediate present while you are ormulating your views, or in the immediate future when you return to Washington and try to translate those views into action. You will not succeed because it is impossible for you to succeed under the system. And it is that pessimistic conclusion which I now will endeavor to demonstrate.

There are just 4 of you and when you get back you will have the task of translating your impressions to, and of convincing something over 400 other Congressmen, just as the 3 Senate Members will endeavor to do to a majority of the other 93 Senators. You and they are sincerely determined to do this. But when you get back and Congress reopens, you will be immersed, you will be submerged, with overwhelming problems of national scope. You will be engrossed and deeply buried in the immediately pressing problems of your own constituencies, your own districts, to which you owe your first and prior obligation. In dealing with Alaskan matters, you will have the gigantic task of transferring your impressions to your numerous colleagues, who will be too busy to give much time to hearing you and very few of whom will have the time to read the full printed record. Even if they do—and a very few possibly may —they will not begin to get the first-hand impressions that you have gotten. And after the 6 months which alone remain of the Eightieth Congress, changes will take place—some of you conceivably will be on other committees, some of you conceivably may not be in Congress the next session.

We have been through this so many times that it is an old story, and, believe me, it is not in the remotest sense a criticism of the individual Members of Congress as such. I believe I have made my conviction on that score clear.

What is it that I think you will not be able to do? In discussing our problems with various members of the two committees, I sense among all of them no dissent whatever from the view that Alaska is destined for statehood and that you are for it. You know that it is right, logical, and just that we should obtain it. You know that it is part of the historic American procedure to grant it to Alaska now that the Alaskans have spoken for it, and that in an official election a substantial majority of them asked for it. But there is some question possibly, among some of the members, whether Alaska is quite "ready" for it. And without in any sense using that term, or that thought, as an excuse to delay or postpone the enactment of statehood, the thought exists among some, a friendly and constructive thought, too, which may be expressed in the following words as they have been expressed to me:

"Why don't you let us help you get ready for statehood? We ought to build you a lot of roads; you haven't got them and you need them."

"Why not let us build you the airfields you haven't got and need?"

"Why not let us build you the hospitals which you ought to have to take care of your tuberculosis cases?"

"Why not let us first help you solve your shipping problem, to get you regular and dependable service, and bring down these excessive freight rates?"

Why not let us dispose of the aboriginal rights issue and clear up the other difficulties in the way of land acquisition so that would-be homesteaders and others may easily acquire a little land on which to build their businesses, tourist lodges, and homes, a procedure which is now so encrusted with red tape and so obstructed by obsolete legislation that your development is hamstrung?

I want to say to you that this is a fine proposal. It would have been a wonderful thing if Congress had years ago undertaken and carried out such a program, and indeed it should have been done. But it has not been. And it will not be done. It will not be done because of the system—the system by which a distant and changing personnel in Congress and in the executive agencies tries through the complexities of government, to help us without giving us the essential tools which alone will enable us to help ourselves. Those tools are two United States Senators and a Representative in the House with a vote.

Let's take roads, for instance. For a quarter of a century, Congress has denied Alaska inclusion under the Federal Highway Act. It has denied us inclusion under any formula whatsoever. Yet I have never met a Member of Congress who visited Alaska, nor any other official visitor, nor indeed any Alaskan, who does not consider that roads are essential to the development of Alaska and that we should have long since had a road-construction program. Nevertheless, year after year, session after session, bills hopefully drawn for that purpose have been lost in the long procession from departmental drafting to final congressional approval. We have not gotten it because, as a Territory, we have not been able to exercise quite enough pressure and mobilize quite enough momentum in the face of more powerful opposed interests, or just plain governmental inertia, to get those bills to enactment.

Is this merely a 25-year-old discrimination, hoary with habit, against which we ceaselessly but vainly rebel? No; there is even more, and more recent. There is a relatively small but highly important part of Alaska which does not come under the provisions of this act; namely, the national forest areas for which Congress has made other provision. In this area, Congress has recently and even more flagrantly discriminated against Alaska. Under the formula covering forest highway allotments, in which Alaska has been included, Alaska's share in the three postwar years, of which this is now the second, should be $2,213,928 per year. Alaska's yearly allocation under this act was arbitrarily cut last year to $1,500,000, thus depriving us of $713,928 a year, or $2,141,784 for the 3-year period. Now, note that this was not an act of economy. This was not a slash made universally in the forest road funds, although these likewise and on top of all this have also been cut for the entire Nation. No; this $2,141,784 was not returned to the Federal Treasury as a benefit for the taxpayer. It was distributed among the 48 States. This was money belonging to Alaska, to which the Alaska Federal income taxpayers had contributed just as did the taxpayers of the 48 States.

The point of this contemporary example is to indicate that the Alaska road situation, as in other Alaska situations, is not merely and only a long-standing injustice which we hope to see rectified, but that right now new discriminations against Alaska are being imposed by the Congress to which you return in the hope of assisting Alaska's development.

Again, I say, there is only one answer, and that is statehood, which would automatically bring our inclusion under the Federal Highway Act and would automatically prevent such discriminations as the cut, for Alaska only, of forest highway funds.

For years, the difficulty of securing title to land has been known to all Alaskans, has been called to the attention of congressional committees who have agreed reform was needed. But nothing happens. It is no better today when thousands of Americans, GI's and others, are clamoring for a chance to settle in Alaska.

Let me give you another example which you probably never heard of. As you have gone through Alaska, you have in many places received complaints about certain of our difficulties—the matter of roads just discussed, the inadequacy of shipping, the need of adequate appropriations to safeguard our salmon supply and wildlife, and much else. And yet in every community you have heard some new problem that you hadn't heard of before. And that, in itself, is an illustration of my point that no congressional committee, even one which works as hard as yours has, can in 2 weeks begin to become acquainted with all of our problems. I might ask, parenthetically, each one of you how you would like it if the solution of your problems in Michigan, in New York, in Illinois, in Utah depended upon the observations and subsequent action of a group of your colleagues taking a 2 weeks' trip to your respective States?

This particular problem which I think is new to you, but old to us, has to do with the administration of justice in Alaska. This is purely a Federal function—we can't do anything about it if we want to. As a Territory, the whole administration of justice has been taken out of our hands by Congress. Way back in the early days of the century, Alaska was divided into four judicial districts because of our vast area. Under each of these four Federal judges whose headquarters are Juneau, Anchorage, Fairbanks, and Nome, there were created United States Commissionerships, held by commissioners—judges, so to speak, of a lesser category—appointed by the judge and located in the smaller communities of Alaska. There are, I believe, about 60 of them. In each of their respective communities, they represent the majesty and might of the United States judicial system. And I think we all agree that the administration of justice—of impartial and speedy justice—

is the cornerstone of our democratic system. These commissioners are unpaid. They derive their total subsistence, except if they have outside jobs, from the fees which they receive incidental to the administering of justice. Only in the four larger towns—Ketchikan, Juneau, Anchorage, and Fairbanks—are these fees sufficient to constitute even a meager livelihood for the commissioners. The result is that, try as the judges will, they often cannot get adequate and worthy commissioners. Some of them, of course, are excellent, often because they have some other means of income, occasionally because a high sense of duty impels them to do the best they can, an arrangement which is grossly unfair to them. But in other places, the persons selected for commissioners, after search for better material proves unavailing and because they are the only persons left in the community who will take the job, are not what they should be. Therefore, the administration of justice suffers, and the repute of the Federal Government suffers, and our whole democratic system suffers.

Now this is not a controversial issue. There is no difference of opinion on this subject anywhere. You have undoubtedly observed that few of the issues that you have encountered in Alaska are not controversial. On these controversial issues, some Alaskans differ with others. But on the commissioner system, everyone agrees that the commissioners should be paid a salary worthy of the importance and dignity of their office, and adequate for a modest livelihood. Ever since I have served the Government, which is now 13 years, efforts have been made to reform this system. In my first weeks as Director of the Division of Territories, I remember that our then Delegate, Anthony J. Dimond, introduced a bill for this purpose. It followed the generally approved formula, approved by both the Department of the Interior and Department of Justice, under which the number of commissioners would be reduced by approximately two-thirds and that these commissioners would be paid a salary. This substantially small number of commissioners would do the work in several towns instead of one because in the smaller communities being a commissioner is not a full-time occupation.

Well, these bills have never passed Congress, chiefly because they involve an appropriation for $100,000 or $150,000. No one particularly opposes them, but they are just not acted upon. Previous to Tony Dimond's effort, Judge Wickersham, who was for many years our Delegate in Congress, tried likewise to secure this legislation. Wickersham was a most distinguished Alaskan; he came here in the early days of the gold rush, was a prospector, miner, explorer, and author; he was a Federal judge, and was early elected a Delegate to Congress where he served for many years. His background and experience all over the Territory rendered him peculiarly qualified to sponsor this type of legislation. But he likewise was unsuccessful. I don't know how far back this effort went, but recently I was reading a book published in 1914 entitled "Ten Thousand Miles With a Dog Sled." It was written by Hudson Stuck, archdeacon of the Yukon, the second-ranking

Episcopalian official in Alaska. The book tells mostly about his travels in remote parts of Alaska in the dog-team days which have largely disappeared. But in the course of his observations, he speaks most critically of the commissioner system, and points out, as our Delegates have subsequently, and as I do now, the inadequacy and disgracefulness of our commissioner system.

As stated, the book was published in 1914, and Archdeacon Stuck states that this "crying evil," as he puts it, has been called to the attention of successive administrations for 20 years. Twenty years before 1914 would take us back to 1894. So we may say that 53 years ago our United States commissioner system was a disgrace, and for 53 years under the Territorial system we have been protesting and trying to get it changed. Just stop and think—1894 was during the administration of President Cleveland—a Democratic administration. Then for the next 16 years we had the Republican administrations of Presidents McKinley, Roosevelt, and Taft. Then we had the Democratic Woodrow Wilson administration for 8 years. Then for 12 years we had the Republican administrations of Harding, Coolidge, and Hoover. Then for the last 15 years we have had a Democratic administration. The country has experienced the "square deal" of President Theodore Roosevelt; the "new freedom" of Woodrow Wilson; the "normalcy" of President Harding; the "New Deal" of President Roosevelt. The world has undergone the greatest transformation it has ever seen in any half century since the beginning of history, but the inexcusable commissioner system of Alaska, which Archdeacon Stuck called vicious over a generation ago, continues unchanged—and it would seem to be almost beyond contradiction, therefore, that it will not be changed until we have two United States Senators whose major duty and responsibility it would be to follow through on these purely Alaskan questions.

Or an alternative would be that under our statehood we should have our own State judicial system and could, therefore, remedy a situation that for 53 years the Federal Government has failed to rectify. This, it seems to me, is typical of a general situation and poses specifically the challenge that if the Federal Government—which means in many cases chiefly the Congress—will not do the things which are obviously indicated in the fields where the Federal Government has exclusive jurisdiction, then it should make possible for Alaska to do the needful, and this can be done only through statehood.

Another instance which may possibly have been called to your attention is the condition of our Federal jails in Alaska. Many of them are loathsome. Perhaps the worst is the Federal jail in Kodiak which, to my knowledge, for at least 20 years, we have been trying to get the Federal Government to replace with a jail fit for human beings. That jail in Kodiak was built in 1898 as a chicken coop and was elevated to the dignity of a jail in 1912, yet the Constitution forbids cruel and unusual punishment. Here 35 years have gone by without appropriate action by the Federal authorities who are exclusively responsible for these Federal jails in Alaska.

Let us take the shipping situation as another example of remote control beyond the power of Alaskans to rectify, but within the power of the Federal authorities, which have not acted.

Because Alaska is American territory we are subject to the coastwise shipping laws. Since maritime transportation to Alaska is interstate commerce, it is likewise beyond the reach of any Alaskan legislative or regulatory body. For years and years the service, which has been a virtual monopoly operating out of Seattle to Alaska, has been inadequate and unsatisfactory, with the rates unduly high and constantly getting higher. The excessiveness of these rates, which at all times have been far higher than any other rates under the flag, have been made the subject of protest by the Alaska Legislature. Those protests have been unheeded. Our experience has shown that these rates issue forth from the Maritime Commission at virtually the behest of the operators. They have been repeatedly issued without hearing, without study, without prior examination of the case of the Alaska consumer and shipper. It has been essentially an ex parte proceeding from start to finish. I won't tire you by going into the long and painful story of how this kind of one-sidedness and total disregard of the Alaska interest in favor of the Seattle monopolists has gone on, except to point out that the situation is not only getting no better but is getting worse. It has reached a point where it is throttling the development of Alaska.

In its present phase the Maritime Commission, after increasing rates about 65 percent at the behest of the carriers and refusing definitely to grant us a hearing before imposing an additional annual $4,000,000 burden on the Alaska consumers, despite every protest also granted this Seattle monopoly the exclusive right to enjoy a new type of subsidy which this Congress, at its last session, voted in order to help Alaska. The Eightieth Congress, conscious of the desperate situation in which Alaska found itself, by joint resolution provided that the operators would be able to get ships for a dollar a year and that the Federal Government would in addition carry the cost of depreciation and insurance on these vessels. During last May and June the Maritime Commission, incidental to the return from Government to private operation, entered into negotiations with the Seattle operators, who had presented an ultimatum, first, that they would not proceed with private operation if there were to be a prior hearing on the substantial rate increases they were demanding; and second, that they would not operate unless they could have an exclusive contract. Before this contract was signed news of it leaked out. A hearing was held in one of the House committee rooms to hear protests. At this were present representatives of Alaska and of business and shipping interests from Portland, San Francisco, and Los Angeles, as well as Members of Congress. A member of the Maritime Commission was also present. It was made clear by the Members of Congress present that it had not been the intent of Congress to bestow these

benefits exclusively on any one operator or group of operators, or
to favor any one American port, but to help Alaska. Senator Guy
Cordon, the senior Senator from Oregon, arose on this occasion
and declared that the proposed exclusive contract would violate the
intent and purpose of Congress and that he deemed it illegal. A
similar view was expressed by Representative Homer Angell, of
Oregon, and Representatives Richard J. Welch, Franck Havenner,
and John J. Allen, Jr., of California. Nevertheless the Maritime
Commission signed this contract. Subsequently it has failed to give
benefits voted by the Congress to an American operator attempting
to establish a much-needed steamship service between Alaska and
Prince Rupert, who is trying to develop a direct and logical route
for midwestern products over direct rail connections from the
Middle West. This American operator, trying to blaze a new trail,
is heavily handicapped and discriminated against in having to buy
his own ships and carry the marine insurance thereon.

Now what is the significance of all this when we deal with perhaps the most important single factor dealing with Alaska's future,
namely, transportation? It means that even the will of Congress,
clearly expressed and recorded, is disregarded as long as Alaska
is not represented in the Congress by two United States Senators
who can follow through on Alaska's needs.

Meanwhile the Jones Act, authored by the late Senator Wesley Jones, of Seattle, enacted in 1920, discriminates exclusively
against Alaska. The United States Supreme Court has admitted
that this discrimination exists, stating that while the act was
discriminatory, Congress has the right to discriminate against a
Territory, a right that it would not have under the Constitution
if Alaska were a State.

So we see in the exclusive discrimination against Alaska in the
Jones Act, and in the exclusively discriminatory assignment of the
congressional subsidy to Seattle operators striking evidence of a
situation of major importance to Alaska and the Nation which will
not be rectified except by statehood. Meanwhile, these astronomic-
al freight rates have driven the cost of living so high in Alaska
that private construction is almost at a standstill and people are
leaving Alaska because living costs have become intolerable.

I might say in passing that this whole issue is confused and
concealed by a species of flag waving which goes under the title
of "Let us build up the American merchant marine."

Surely, we're all in favor of building up the American merchant marine, but let us analyze what it means in this case. The
American merchant marine in the case of the Alaska trade is
largely one individual who is the chief owner of the two principal
lines having this monopoly, the Alaska Steamship Co. and the
Northland Transportation Co. The third and smaller company, the
Alaska Transportation Co., has already denounced the contract
of which it was a minor beneficiary, and is requesting the Maritime Commission to cancel the contract with itself and the two
larger one-man-owned companies on the ground that it cannot
get a fair allocation of ships and that the limited Alaskan routes

assigned to it have already been invaded, contrary to the agreement, by one of the other two larger steamship lines.

It is obvious that the development of Alaska, an area one-fifth as large as the United States, is now of paramount strategic importance and is far more urgent than this local so-called development of the American merchant marine which is nothing more than the financial enhancement of one individual.

This seems to me an illustration of the third point which I stressed at the beginning of my testimony, namely, that you will not be able to succeed in doing for us the things you believe should be done and that you want to do. You will not, I reluctantly prophesy, be able to free us from the grip of the shipping octopus and secure us adequate shipping at reasonable rates. Two United States Senators from Alaska would, I am confident, go far to help you do it.

And I wish to point out finally that the shipping situation is worse today than it ever has been.

Let us now turn to another striking example—Alaska's major industry, salmon fishing. The regulations for its management have been exclusively under Federal control since the Organic Act of 1912, a Federal control reaffirmed by the White Act in 1924. Under these and other acts, Congress has reserved to the Federal Government the exclusive right to regulate and conserve our fisheries. The justification advanced for this distant control of an Alaska resource is that salmon is such a great and important national asset that the Nation cannot risk its depletion through Territorial control and management. So that although for years the Territorial legislature has memorialized Congress to turn over this function to the Territory, Congress has turned a deaf ear.

Now, what has happened under this joint Federal legislative and Federal executive control? The salmon runs have steadily gone down. So serious is the situation in southeastern Alaska that its people have been warned by the Fish and Wildlife Service that certain areas may be totally closed to commercial fishing next year. You have heard the uncontradicted testimony of all sorts of people in Alaska, representatives of the canned-salmon industry, of fishermen, trollers, purse-seiners, gill-netters, and others, that the salmon fisheries were being depleted and that one reason for their depletion was that Congress never appropriated enough money to see that the fishing grounds, all of which lie in Territorial waters, were properly patrolled and guarded against poaching and illicit fishing of all kinds. Here also the situation is getting worse because not only are the runs of fish becoming steadily smaller but because at this time we are dealing with an economy-minded Congress. If during the prosperous twenties of Coolidge and Hoover and the presumably generous New Deal days sufficient money was not appropriated to safeguard this great national asset, what is to be hoped for with a Congress that is determined to cut Federal expenditures lower than they have been?

It is true that we cannot prophesy exactly what would be done if this prime national asset were turned over to Alaska, but I can assure you that Alaska could not do worse or as badly as has been done. Alaska's people here are vitally concerned with the preservation of salmon. It is the livelihood directly or indirectly of nearly all the people living on the coast of Alaska. It is vital —to the economy of Ketchikan, Wrangell, Petersburg, Sitka, Juneau, Haines, and of a dozen other communities largely inhabited by natives whose livelihood is almost exclusively derived from the sea—Metlakatla, Craig, Klawock, Angoon, Kake, Hoonah, and Yakutat.

Again I ask you, will you be able to rectify this situation when you get back to the opening of the second session of the Eightieth Congress? Will you be able to reverse, and in this case run counter to the general economy trend, and provide Alaska with the funds necessary for enforcement? I fear not. By giving us statehood, you will have the best chance in the world of solving this acute and major problem also.

Let us take another important field of activity, one upon which the future stability and permanence of a large part of Alaska depends—agriculture. It is well known that agriculture, wherever established, means permanence. The farmer, if he can make a living, is a permanent dweller, and he gives stability to the community around him. The stability which agriculture would furnish is much needed in Alaska. Its development would likewise be effective in holding down the cost of living by supplying at lower prices commodities whose costs are high because of long hauls and high shipping rates. Alaska could supply most of the food that it needs for its own maintenance. It could supply its own beef, its own pork products, its lamb and mutton, its own dairy products, its own chickens and eggs, and most of its vegetables. Likewise, it is clear that tens of thousands of Americans, many of them ex-GI's, would like to come to Alaska to farm. Thousands of letters bear testimony to that desire. It is also apparent that strategically and economically such a migration, and such settlement would be highly desirable.

Now, it is also clear that, given the relatively virginal condition of Alaska agriculture, Alaskan farmers, actual and potential, need the kind of assistance that agricultural research can give them. Congress recognized that long ago in the 48 States. In Alaska this need is even greater because our farmers operate in different latitudes, in different climates, and with different soils from those in the States. The experience in the States, therefore, gathered through its numerous agricultural experiment stations, is not applicable to Alaska. Now for years and years, we have tried to secure adequate appropriations for agricultural research in Alaska. Not only have we not succeeded, but Congress has repeatedly denied us the funds that we were entitled to under its own acts. This is all the more striking in that we know that just across Bering Sea the Soviet Government is spending vast sums in agricultural research and development, extending the limits of agriculture further and further north, developing new strains of grain, devising new agricultural methods, and establishing an increasing permanent population there. Where is Congress's concern for the national interest, let alone Alaska's interest?

I referred to this in my earlier testimony, pointing out in detail under what acts having to do with agriculture, Alaska had failed to get its share under the formulas established by Congress and that the sums thus denied Alaska would to date total some $13,000,000. I refer you to my earlier estimony on this subject and bring it up now again only because even in the less than 6 months since I testified, the situation has become incredibly worse—if that were possible. For Congress, by an act unprecedented in its arbitrariness, has moved in and taken over the agricultural experiment station of the University of Alaska and appropriated, or rather I should say "expropriated" for use by the Federal Department of Agriculture such funds as the Territory appropriated for the conducting of the station. It did this, moreover, without the approval of the Secretary of Agriculture and over the protest of our Delegate and the university authorities.

It may be hard perhaps for you to believe this, but it happened during and was done by the Congress of which you are Members. To sum up what has happened, Congress has consistently denied Alaska funds to which the Territory was entitled by Congress' own acts appropriating funds for agricultural research for land-grant colleges, and now has gone one step beyond and has expropriated Alaska's own funds for that purpose.

Will you be able to reverse the action of the Congress of which you have been a part? It hardly seems likely.

The discriminations against Alaska which continue during the years, and are growing worse rather than better at the very time when Alaska should be the object of special solicitude and attention by the Congress, have to do with both legislation and appropriations, and the two are often inseparably linked. These discriminations fall into two categories: first, those in which Alaska is specifically discriminated against such as in the failure to include Alaska in the Federal Highway Act, the reduction affecting Alaska only in the Forest Highway Act, the failure to appropriate sufficient money for fishery and wildlife protection, the failure to appropriate money for agriculture under specific acts of Congress; and second, and no less important, but somewhat less obvious, the discriminations against Alaska administratively following the reduction of funds for an administrative agency's over-all program. I could cite as contemporary examples of this latter discrimination the cuts by Congress of the CAA program, the result of which falls most heavily in Alaska where aviation development is of greater relative importance than elsewhere, the virtual elimination of the appropriations for our fishery products laboratory in Ketchikan, through the reduction of the over-all program of experimental laboratories operated by the Fish and Wildlife Service, and the elimination of the Alaska Coast Guard district.

When the administrative agencies operating throughout the Nation find themselves obliged to reduce, we Alaskans know in advance where the reduction is coming, and it comes largely, we know, because we do not have the political strength that two Senators would give us. Our Delegate is not in a position to do more than plead.

I want to point out incidentally in the case of our fishery products laboratory in Ketchikan that it is supported jointly by the Territory and Federal Government. The Federal contribution to it has amounted to only some $30,000 a year, and the laboratory has, in its 10 years of operation, already produced products through research which more than repay its costs through increased economic activity in the processing and marketing of new products which in turn pay Federal income taxes. Cutting off this laboratory in Alaska where there are still vast untapped and undeveloped fisheries (other than salmon and halibut) is the type of economy that isn't economy at all. Not merely Alaska but the whole Nation is the poorer in consequence. Two Alaska Senators would, I believe, have prevented it.

But let me take the Coast Guard as a specific example. Before this last session of Congress, the Coast Guard had 14 districts. As a result of the economy wave, it now has 12. One of the two eliminated was the Alaska district with headquarters located in Ketchikan. The present district headquarters are situated in Boston, New York, Norfolk, Miami, St. Louis, Cleveland, New Orleans, Long Beach, Calif., San Francisco, Seattle, San Juan, Puerto Rico, and Honolulu. The consolidations that were made consisted in closing the Philadelphia office and consolidating it with the New York office 100 miles away, and abolishing the Ketchikan headquarters and moving it to Seattle.

How incredible this administrative action was may be gathered from a few facts that I am now going to give you.

Alaska has a coastline of 26,000 miles. Alaska's coastline is 7,000 miles longer than the entire coast line of the United States including the Atlantic, the Gulf, and the Pacific coasts.

The Coast Guard is far more important in the life of Alaska than in the life of any State. Consider, for instance, the importance of the Guard in any State with a long coast line like California, and you will find that not one citizen in a hundred in that great State, possibly not one in 500, is personally interested and directly concerned with the work of the Coast Guard. Only if he is a fisherman or possibly a yachtsman, or connected with some coastwise shipping operation is he interested in the Coast Guard and in its work.

But in Alaska, everyone except the miner makes his living from the sea, and the Coast Guard is an agency which is vital to the majority of Alaskans and they depend upon it. I am glad to record that no Federal agency in the past has served the people of Alaska more effectively and is more highly esteemed than the United States Coast Guard. I hate to see that service shattered as it now will be.

Moreover, in addition to the greater day-in day-out service which the Coast Guard renders in Alaska, it performs several other functions in Alaska, which are unique and peculiar to Alaska.

Annually, the Coast Guard convoys the fur seals in their migration to the Pribilof Islands, protecting them the entire way against destruction by pelagic sealing. Annually, also, the Coast Guard goes on the well known "court cruise" when it carries the personnel of the Federal District Court of the Third Judicial Division, the judge, United States attorney, marshal, clerk of court, secretaries, and others, along the Alaska Peninsula and through the Aleutians.

Finally, the coast of Alaska is the stormiest of all the American coasts, is not as completely charted and wire-dragged as the other American coast lines, and presents therefore special hazards which require more, rather than less attention. It just seems unthinkable that the Alaska Coast Guard district should not have been allowed to remain as one of the 12 which continue even after the drastic economies by the Eightieth Congress.

Under the present arrangement by which the Alaska district headquarters were abolished and relegated to Seattle, the direction and command for the Alaska operations is at a point 700 miles south of Alaska's southernmost boundary where Alaska's 26,000 mile coast line begins.

There is yet more. Alaska is a highly strategic area. During World War II, a war fought against Japan, the Army freed Alaska from its control from the Presidio in San Francisco and created a Department of Alaska with headquarters at Anchorage.

The Navy likewise changed Alaska from a subsector of the Thirteenth Naval District with headquarters at Seattle and created of Alaska a Seventeenth Naval District with headquarters at Kodiak. The autonomy of both the Army's and Navy's command in Alaska continues. Given the Coast Guard's close relationship to national defense, it is preposterous that the Alaska Coast Guard district be abolished and its command removed 700 miles farther away than it was.

Now it is true that Congress did not specifically order this particular retrenchment. But it might just as well have done so. Long experience has taught us that the administrative agencies, which of course depend upon Congress for their funds, follow the cue which Congress itself gives them. The high command in the Coast Guard would not dare, except for the most obvious and patent reasons, abolish a district represented by two United States Senators who, upon hearing the first rumor of such intending abolition, would descend upon Coast Guard headquarters with set jaws and an "or else" in their curt comment.

Given all the above-cited importance of the Coast Guard to Alaska, it seems hard to believe that California with a coast line of only 900 miles, would retain two Coast Guard district headquarters, and Alaska none. A proper allocation of Coast Guard headquarters would not only not deprive Alaska of its established district headquarters, but would probably give Alaska two or three such districts. However, we'd be glad to settle for one—the one that has been taken from us.

Can you rectify this? It has already happened, and it is no

paper transfer. What was formerly the Alaska district headquarters in Ketchikan has been stripped of personnel and equipment, so that it will not be able properly to carry out its functions. Here is a direct injury to national policy, national safety, as well as national interest, besides the Alaska interest, which only two Senators, the two Alaska Senators which statehood will give us, could have averted.

I will touch upon one more major discrimination, which likewise injures not merely Alaska but the national interest. Tuberculosis is the most serious menace to the health of Alaska and to its population growth.

The death rate in Alaska from tuberculosis is nine times what it is in the 48 States and approaches that of India and China. India and China, I might say in passing, are receiving or will receive, as are 50 or more foreign countries, all kinds of substantial financial aid from Uncle Sam's Treasury. Tuberculosis is destroying our population. Five persons die of tuberculosis every week in Alaska. The disease is spreading. It is spreading because it is a contagious disease and every active case of tuberculosis transmits the sickness to others. It is increasing because the Federal Government, despite the most earnest appeals, has failed to do its duty in the matter of appropriations. And the problem is wholly one of appropriations utilized for hospital beds. Give us the beds and we will stop the advance of tuberculosis.

Although the greater part of these tuberculosis cases are among the so-called native—Eskimo and Indian—population which have been and are, in matters of health, education, and welfare, a Federal responsibility, the tubercle bacilli are not respecters of race. They are spreading their infection and infecting more and more people, native and white alike. The economic loss, when substantially over 5 percent of the population is ill with this disease, is a further handicap to Alaska's development and a costly and wasteful drain on the Nation's economy. Besides actually incapacitating Alaskans and removing them by death, the rising menace of tuberculosis is causing people to leave the Territory who would otherwise remain, and is discouraging others from coming. Moreover here is an example of where the Territory has, it seems to me, done its part. In a special session of the Territorial legislature which I called in 1946, an appropriation of $250,000 for the care of tuberculosis sufferers was voted for the coming years, and a $440,000 appropriation for the biennium was voted at the regular session in 1947. Meanwhile the pleas for a corresponding action by the Federal Government, though voted by the United States House of Representatives was rejected by the United States Senate. Alaska was represented in the House by a Delegate, and he managed to persuade the House to act. But there was no Alaska Senator to bring about corresponding action in the Senate.

Gentlemen of the House Subcommittee on Territories, is it not fair to ask you whether you can remove these outstanding handicaps to Alaska's welfare and happiness, to its stability and growth?

I regret that I have to reiterate my belief that you cannot, and that the only way you can help us to rectify all of them at one time is to give yourselves the assistance two Senators from the State of Alaska would give you. It would be their exclusive task to work for these measures. It is far, far from your exclusive task to do anything of the kind.

Much of what I have said would seem to indicate my conviction that it is the absence of the political influence and political strength which two Senators and a voting Representative would supply that has caused these problems to fester unsolved through the years and to grow worse, not better. And that, I believe, is palpably and demonstrably true. But from a mere mechanical standpoint, consider how virtually impossible, how next to super-human, is the task imposed on one Delegate, voteless or otherwise. How well would your problems in Michigan, New York, Illinois, and Utah be handled if you had only one man in Congress to work at them? When a problem of vital concern affects the State of Michigan, Representative Crawford, you can, if necessary, call for assistance on 2 Senators and 16 other Representatives, a total of 19 to perform the work that for Alaska has to be done by one man.

If and when you, Representative LeFevre, and your colleagues meet a proposition coming up in Congress which you deem injurious to the great Empire State, some 45 Congressmen can back up your 2 Senators to fight for or against the issue—a total of 47.

In Illinois, Representative Jenison, there would be 27 of you.

Even in Utah, Representative Dawson, with only two Representatives, there are at least four of you.

To present the needs and to fight the battles of the largest political entity under the flag, Alaska has just one man. He, Delegate Bartlett, is an extremely devoted and capable man and Alaska is most fortunate in having him. The people of Alaska have shown their appreciation of his indefatigable service. For after electing him the first time by a majority of just under 2 to 1, they returned him last year by a majority of nearly 3 to 1. But he is just one man, and there are only 24 hours a day. Many times when in Washington, I have seen how Alaska problems came up before four or five different House committees, meeting simultaneously, where it was a manifest physical impossibility for a Delegate to be present before all of them. He must endeavor to compensate for his singleness and spend much extra time of his already insufficient time trying to arrange to have some friendly Members of Congress as a favor present his case and plead his cause before the committee meetings which he is not able to attend personally. Then, if favorable action follows, he must leave his work in the House to go to the other side of the Capitol and try to repeat the performance in the Senate. That is scarcely fair to Alaska or the Nation; nor can it be considered efficient.

In addition to that, the lone Delegate has to carry on all the work with the multitude of departments, bureaus, agencies of the executive branch of the Government.

Gentlemen, there is only one answer. There is only one way

in which you can help us effectively. Give us statehood and give us and yourselves the help that a minimum delegation in the Congress of two Senators and one Representative would bring.

So to recapitulate, when there are those who either because they wish to delay statehood say, "We are not ready for it," or those others who believe in statehood as elementary justice and our natural right, but wonder, as some of you may have, whether it might not be better to have a short intervening period before statehood is granted, a period in which, theoretically, we would be made "readier" for statehood, a period in which all these various things which we have not been able to achieve for 80 years under the American flag would be done for us by the Congress, I say to you that we will never be "readier" for statehood until we get statehood. I say to you that, on the contrary, this government by remote control, this government by distant absentees, this government by a changing personnel in Congress and by changing bureau heads, however well-intentioned, however well-meaning, makes us daily less fit for statehood. We shall never be any more ready for statehood than we are now. We shall never be any more ready for statehood until we get statehood. The record makes that abundantly clear.

Finally, you have heard a good deal about what statehood will do for Alaska, but little or nothing has been said about what Alaska statehood will do for the United States.

Alaska has a real contribution to make to the councils of the Nation. Our unique geographical position—the only part of the country which extends westward into the Eastern Hemisphere and northward far beyond the Arctic Circle—gives us a closeness, a knowledge, and a stake in the great problems of the Pacific area. If Alaska had had two Senators 10 years ago, this continent would never have been invaded, and the Japs would never have held American islands for a year, really winning the Aleutian campaign by sacrificing a few expendables, and containing thereby tens of thousands of American troops and vast amounts of shipping, matériel, and supplies. Our Delegate in Congress, able and far-sighted Anthony J: Dimond, repeatedly warned and foretold what would and did happen. But a voteless Delegate's warnings go unheeded. Many American boys' lives—lives lost in the Aleutians—would have been saved had Alaska been a State prior to World War II:

But what of the future? The Pacific is the ocean of the coming century just as the Atlantic was the great ocean during the four centuries after the discovery of America, and as the Mediterranean was in ancient times. Alaska's shore line on the Pacific is greater than that of our other three Pacific coast States—Washington, Oregon, and California. Our coast extends to within naked-eye visibility of Asia from which will arise some of our greatest and most pressing problems in the generations to come.

In addition to that, Alaska alone fronts on the Arctic, now generally assumed to be the great airways of the future. Our familiarity with what to most other Americans are remote and unknown regions will be of inestimable value in shaping national policies. Great events in the immediate future will take place not far from Alaska's doorsteps. They will affect the whole future of the United States and, indeed, of the whole world. But Alaska's interest and insight will be earlier, closer, keener. And our Nation will be safer and stronger by availing itself thereof to the fullest extent.

But this is not the only contribution which Alaska can make in the legislative halls of the Union. Alaska, in part still the last frontier, is inhabited by the pioneer type of American who built America and made it the great and dynamic country that it is today. In the earlier, settled, longer established, older parts of the United States, some of that spirit of youth and vigor which once was everywhere in America has diminished, perhaps petered out. We still have it in Alaska. Alaskans are the independent thinking, hard-working, robust breed which we like to think of, and properly, as characteristically American. They came to Alaska, just as in an earlier day other Americans moved west, to hew for themselves a living in a battle with nature. That spirit and that character should, for the whole Nation's good, be represented with a voice and a vote at both ends of the Capitol.''

While the hearings at Barrow, Nome, Kodiak and Cordova were not recorded, summaries were made by Chairman Crawford. One of his comments on Barrow has a subsequent relevance:

"In visiting some of the homes we had a chance to acquaint ourselves with the positively terrible conditions under which some of the natives live. As many as 8 or 10 people live in homes consisting of no more than one or two small rooms with more or less the members of the family diseased with active TB and adults, children and young dogs—puppies—all sleeping in the same room. It is my frank opinion that the United States Government is participating in a positively terrible program by permitting conditions to exist as we found in Point Barrow. The whole situation is inexcusable and it should be corrected without further delay.''

The subsequent relevance lies in the fact that while this ''inexcusable situation'' was not ''corrected without further delay'' during the remaining eleven years of territorialism, under statehood, through the efforts of Senator Bartlett, natural gas was piped in to heat the Barrow homes and Bartlett's bill to provide adequate housing in Eskimo communities was enacted by the 89th Congress as an amendment to the Demonstration Cities Act of 1966.

While no action on the statehood bill took place on the House floor, because of the opposition of the Majority Leader, Joseph W. Martin, Jr., R., of Massachusetts, the favorable reports of the Subcommittee and full Committee constituted a gratifying start toward statehood.

Dorothy Gruening happily displays the front page of the Anchorage *Times* with its in-spired headline, "We're In," to no-less happy Alaska-Tennessee Plan Senator and Mrs. William A. Egan.

MEANWHILE; President Truman wrote a unique chapter in American history by sending, on May 21, 1948, a long message to Congress devoted wholly to Alaska. In it he revealed a great understanding of Alaska's needs and problems to help meet which he urged Congress to take various steps designed to insure the success of Alaskan statehood, and he again urged as "the most important action the government can take." No similar document is to be found in the record of Presidential messages, although there were previous instances of White House support for the admission of a particular State. It helped the statehood cause immensely.

In the 81st Congress, Bob Bartlett introduced another statehood bill, H. R: 331. Only one day's hearing was given to it on the ground that the previous year's hearing on an almost identical bill, H. R. 206, would suffice. H. R. 331, however, was in some respects, an improved version in that it gave the prospective State four sections of land in each township numbered 2, 16, 32 and 36, instead of only 16 and 36, as well as Section 33 in the Tanana Valley for the University of Alaska.

In executive session, with Clair Engle, Democrat, of California, presiding, the bill was again reported on March 8, 1949.

This Alaska bill came up on the floor a year later, March 3, 1950, and was passed by a vote of 186 to 146, with 100 not voting. The debate lasted one day. Those voicing support for it were: J. Hardin Peterson, D., of Florida; Fred Crawford, R., of Michigan; Homer Angell, R., of Oregon; John E. Miles, D., of New Mexico; Fred Marshall, D., of Minnesota; Gordon L. McDonough, R., of California; Mike Mansfield, D., of Montana; Jacob Javits, R., of New York; Gordon Canfield, R., of New Jersey; Victor Wickersham, D., of Oklahoma; Usher Burdick, R., of North Dakota; Wayne Aspinall, D., of Colorado; Barratt O'Hara, D., of Illinois; Hale Boggs, D., of Louisiana; John McCormack, D., of Mass.; Reva Basone, D., of Utah; Roy W. Wier, D., of Minnesota; John R. Murdock, D., of Arizona; and Frank B. Keefe, R., of Wisconsin.

Those expressing opposition were: Harold D. Cooley, D., of North Carolina; Justin L. Johnson, R., of California; Thomas G. Abernethy, D., of Mississippi; James J. Delaney, D., of New York; Walter B. Huber, D., of Ohio; Herbert C. Bonner, D., of North Carolina; Clare E. Hoffman, R., of Michigan; and Joseph P. O'Hara, R., of Minnesota.

A. L. Miller, R., of Nebraska, sought to amend the bill to provide that instead of granting Alaska 4 out of 36 sections, which would give the new State about 12 per cent of its total area, the State should receive all the even numbered sections, which would give the new State close to half of the total area, making allowance for the Federal withdrawals which would not be affected. He had sought to introduce that amendment in committee. The amendment was opposed by Delegate Bartlett[1] and J: Hardin Peterson, who was in charge of the bill, as contrary to previous practice in western states and bound to incur the Federal government's opposition. When his amendment was defeated, Miller voted against the bill. The debate was concluded with a strong plea by Delegate Bartlett.

The Hawaii statehood bill came up in the House on March 6th and was debated extensively that day. The next day, March 7, 1950, it passed by a vote of 262 to 110.

The Senate hearings were scheduled to begin on April 24th. Considering the importance of the first Senate hearing on the statehood bill, I sought for a way to get it off to a good start. So I telephoned Earl Warren, Governor of California, the previous week and asked him if he could attend the first hearing and be one of the witnesses. I had gotten to know him not only through the national Governors' Conferences, but at the regional

Governor Ernest Gruening testifying at first statehood hearing before United States Senate in the Senate Committee on Interior and Insular Affairs. April 29, 1950. Senators from left to right: Hugh Butler (R) of Nebraska, Clinton Anderson (D) of New Mexico, Glen Taylor (D) of Idaho, Zales Ecton (R) of Montana. Immediately back of Hugh Butler is Alice Freyn Johnson, correspondent for the Seattle *Times*.

Conferences of Western Governors, which were somewhat more intimate and informal affairs. After the Governors' Conference in Salt Lake City in 1947, eleven governors, including Earl Warren and I, had accepted an invitation by Secretary of the Navy James Forrestal, who wanted to interest the governors in the Naval R.O.T.C., to travel to Hawaii on the battleship "Iowa." A five-day cruise enables one to get to know one's traveling companions well, and with the three subsequent days in Hawaii had exposed these governors to the reasons for statehood for both these Pacific territories.

Secretary of the Interior, Oscar L. Chapman, and Governor Earl Warren of California, witnesses at first Senate statehood hearing, reading the pamphlet, "Eighty-three Years of Neglect," compiled by Evangeline Atwood of Anchorage.

Without a moment's hesitation, that great, generous American asked: "When do you want me?" I said: "The hearing begins at 10 a.m. next Monday." "I'll be there," said Earl.

He arrived earlier that morning. I met him at the Washington airport and together we went to the Interior Committee's room in the Capitol. Committee members present were: Clinton P. Anderson, D., of New Mexico; Glen H. Taylor, D., of Idaho; Herbert H. Lehman, D., of New York; Hugh Butler, R., of Nebraska; Guy Cordon, R., of Oregon; Zales N. Ecton, D., of Montana.

Senator Anderson called the meeting to order, explaining that of the members senior to him, Senator O'Mahoney was ill, Senator Murray's wife was critically ill, Senator Downey was also ill, and Senator McFarland was chairing a crime hearing. I learned later that President Truman had especially requested Senator Anderson to conduct the hearings.

The first witness was Oscar L. Chapman, Secretary of the Interior, who had just succeeded Julius Krug. He reaffirmed the Truman administration's support of statehood for Alaska and Hawaii and urged "prompt and favorable action. . . .on the Alaska statehood bill."

Governor Earl Warren spoke extemporaneously and with moving eloquence.

Later, when I asked how much we owed him for his transportation, pointing out that the Statehood Committee had funds for such a purpose, he declined to accept reimbursement, saying: "It's been a pleasure." He returned to California immediately after his testimony, having come for just that purpose.

But before leaving the hearing, in response to a question by Senator Anderson as to how Governor Warren felt about Hawaii, he gave its statehood cause no less firm support than he had given Alaska's.

The next witness, Lt. General Nathan F. Twining, of the Air Force, then Commander-in-Chief of the Alaskan Command, testified that in his view "statehood for Alaska would help the military. . . .and be a great asset to military development."

Father Bernard R. Hubbard, S.J., known as "the Glacier Priest," who had spent much time in Alaskan exploration, was under obligations to some salmon cannery men who had helped finance his expeditions, was expected to testify against statehood. But two Alaskan priests, Father Edgar Gallant and Father Paul C. O'Connor, S.J., had taken him aside as the hearing began and given him a dressing-down, so that his testimony was neither pro nor con except for voicing a fear that under statehood the burden of taxation would fall on so few.

Assistant Secretary of State John D. Hickerson, testified to the Department's favorableness of statehood.

Judge Anthony Dimond made a masterful presentation of the case for statehood.

Vermont-born Robert E. Ellis, who had lived 21 years in Alaska, Mayor of Ketchikan, former Alaskan bush pilot who had founded and was manager of Ellis Airlines, appeared "as a businessman", saying:

> "The arguments we hear presented against statehood are similar to the arguments that faced us when we started in business in Alaska. The cards were stacked against us, but we managed to overcome those obstacles. We can do that in Alaska.
> "That same spirit, that same faith, that same courage that enabled us to make a success of our business in Alaska is going to enable us to make a success of the business of running the State of Alaska."

He was followed by William L. Baker, Editor and Publisher of the Ketchikan Chronicle, who ably gave a variety of examples of how territorial status disadvantaged Alaska.

Although I was scheduled to be the last witness, I was unexpectedly called upon to answer a question raised by Senator Ecton, of Montana, concerning action by the Interior Department in reserving a 600-foot right of way along the Alaska Highway, 300 feet along primary roads, and 200 along secondary roads. Under the provisions of H. R. 331, this land, having been reserved, would remain in Federal ownership under statehood. This action had been scathingly attacked as "fantastic" by Delegate Bartlett in a letter to Secretary Krug, and had also been condemned by the Interior Department's own field committee in Alaska, but nevertheless had not been voided by the Interior Department on orders of Assistant Secretary William E. Warne. This was, I pointed out, the type of bureaucratic and arbitrary action by Federal agencies of which the people of Alaska were the victims and made us want statehood.[2] I then cited other similar examples, and of Alaskans' constant struggle against such actions.

Zachary Loussac, Anchorage businessman and the city's Mayor, stressed Alaska's need for self-government.

Irene Ryan, Alaska's only woman mining engineer, pointed to the difficulties of getting investment capital into a Territory.

At the second day's hearing, Mrs. Mildred Hermann, attorney, former O.P.A. Director, one of two Alaska's women lawyers, and Secretary of the Alaska Statehood Commission, testified effectively at great length on the question: "Can Alaska support statehood?" It was a masterful presentation with facts and figures concerning revenues and costs. Statehood was possible, as it had not been at the time of earlier House hearings because, as Mrs. Hermann, referring to the legislation adopted by the 1949 legislature, pointed out: "Now, in the past year, Alaska has put its tax system and its finances in order and, in doing so, it has anticipated statehood. Today we may talk in terms of a sound, existing tax structure, not something that we are going to do in the future, but what we have already done in the past."

One passage in Mildred Hermann's testimony was to be widely quoted. In response to questioning as to whether, under statehood, Alaska could afford all its people hoped for, Mrs. Hermann said:

> "If we cannot buy steak, we will eat beans. We will fit the pattern to the cloth. If we cannot make the kind of a dress we want, we will make one that will cover us anyway, and we are perfectly willing to pull in our belts and do without some things for the purpose of statehood."

Of course, this was common sense and realism which typified the spirit of the statehood advocates, but Mildred's "We will eat beans" became the phrase with which statehood foes twitted its friends.

J. T. Sanders, legislative counsel of the National Grange, testified to his organization's support of the statehood bill. The Grange, he pointed out, was organized in 1867, the year of Alaska's purchase.

"Thus, for the entire life-time of our order, Alaska has been a disenfranchised part of our nation. It seems to me totally unjustifiable that the inhabitants of the important part of the nation, the world's leading and most powerful democracy, should have been deprived of full citizenship rights for these 84 years."

The Reverend G. Edgar Gallant, of Skagway, whom I had appointed to the Territorial Board of Public Welfare, the first priest ever ordained in Alaska and its senior priest by 6 years, testified that "the majority of real Alaskans are for statehood."

In reply to a question from Senator Ecton whether Father Gallant realized that once an enabling act had been consented to it was irrevocable, he replied:

"I think I understand that pretty well because the profession I am now in I am in for life", at which there was laughter.

The third day of the hearings began with the testimony of Governor Alfred E. Driscoll, of New Jersey. Stating that he had traveled extensively through Alaska, Governor Driscoll said:

> "First consideration undoubtedly should be given to the pressing issue of national defense. Alaska must be defended by the United States and today Alaska lacks adequate defense. It is not only in the field of national defense that the Territory occupies a strategic area. . . .Alaska may be considered one of the most important proving grounds for our republic. Here is an area in which we have an opportunity to demonstrate the capacity of our republic, to put its ideals and principles into practical operation. In other words, we have an opportunity to put our avowed ideals of home rule and representative government to work. The most effective offensive that our nation could take in the present world crisis is for us to demonstrate its capacity for continuing growth and to further demonstrate its capacity to put its principles and ideals to work in this vast frontier land."

John C. Williams, representing the Veterans of Foreign Wars, testified that that organization had repeatedly gone on record urging statehood for Alaska.

Marvin T. Goldberger, representing the American Veterans of World War II, (Amvets), testified to that organization's support of statehood.

In questioning Edward V. Davis, attorney, representing the Anchorage Chamber of Commerce, the committee now turned from probing the general Alaska sentiment for statehood to whether H. R. 331 was a satisfactory bill. Davis's position was that while Alaskans would like as generous terms as they could get, they preferred prompt action on this bill, which had already passed the House. Senator Anderson took exception to this position and insisted that it was the Senate's duty to scrutinize the bill closely, and to improve it.

W. D. Johnson, Vice-President of the Order of Railway Conductors, submitted a statement in behalf of the Railway Labor Executives Association, consisting of twenty standard railway labor organizations, in favor of statehood. The organizations were:

Brotherhood of Locomotive Firemen and Enginemen
Order of Railway Conductors of America
Switchmen's Union of North America

Order of Railroad Telegraphers
American Train Dispatchers' Association
International Association of Machinists
International Brotherhood of Boilermakers, Iron Ship Builders and
  Helpers of America
International Brotherhood of Blacksmiths, Drop Forgers and Helpers
Sheet Metal Workers International Association
International Brotherhood of Electrical Workers
Brotherhood of Railway Carmen of America
International Brotherhood of Firemen and Oilers
Brotherhood of Railway and Steamship Clerks, Freight Handlers,
  Express and Station Employees
Brotherhood of Maintenance of Way Employees
Brotherhood of Railroad Signalmen of America
National Organization Masters, Mates and Pilots of America
National Marine Engineers' Beneficial Association
International Longshoremen's Association
Hotel and Restaurant Employees and Bartenders International Union
Railroad Yardmasters of America

Gunnard Engebreth, Territorial Senator, President of the Senate, representing himself and the Anchorage Republican Club, testifying for statehood, expressed the view that the assumption that if Alaska were admitted to statehood it would send Democrats to Congress was not necessarily correct. He cited the close division between the parties in the 1949 legislature, where, after a prolonged deadlock, a Democrat, Frank Peratrovich, was elected President of the Senate for the special session, and he, a Republican, had been elected President of the regular session. (He was again elected President of the Senate for the 1951 legislature.)

George Sundborg, manager of the Alaska Development Board, gave a detailed and knowledgeable account of the still undeveloped or under-developed resources that statehood could stimulate—the minerals, the fisheries other than salmon and halibut, timber, tourists, petroleum, hydro-power.

"Alaska is still only at the very beginning of its development," he said. "We have wealth here which has waited, waited and waited to be utilized, and I think it has waited and waited for a number of reasons, one of which has been what kind of government we have in that part of the world;" and, concluding:

"I think that Alaska constitutes a new West, and it can be just as important to the growth and expansion and economic well-being of the United States as the West was in earlier years. . . .Our history has been that our areas are developed when we place in the hands of the people of those areas the tools of government they need in order to run their own affairs, and that areas become great under statehood; they do not become great under territorialism."

Delegate Bartlett followed with a comprehensive recital of the justification for statehood, saying:

"Second-class citizenship is what Alaskans now have. . . ."
"I have often said, and repeat here, if any Alaskan would stay with me for one week and make the ceaseless rounds with me,

thereby learning as he could not otherwise what inferior status a Territory has, he would become a proponent and rather an active one of this statehood cause."

". . . .The chief opposition against statehood will be placed before this committee by the salmon industry. That industry is not entitled to have a dominant voice in deciding what the status of Alaska shall be. There is nothing new, however, in a great industry seeking to block statehood. On the contrary, that has been the usual pattern throughout the West. But when statehood came, industry found that the true American form of government was not too bad after all. . . ."

"That industry is bleeding with sympathy for Alaska. The statehood bill before you, it is alleged, does not give the new State sufficient land. This is asserted in very dramatic fashion by impressive arrays of figures appearing on and around maps of Alaska.

"Do you think the salmon industry, opposed to statehood in any form, cares at all how much land is granted in the bill? Of course not. It has seized upon this issue only because it believes it will be a popular one and one which might attract sympathetic attention both in Congress and in Alaska. I have a suspicion that if the statehood bill granted 50 per cent of all the land to the State, the salmon industry would be before you protesting the national interest was being violated by such a radical departure from the formula heretofore adopted. And if the land issue weren't to the fore, the salmon industry would raise some other point in an attempt to make it an issue."

". . . .The chief objection of those principally concerned with taking Alaska's salmon is that they fear the people of Alaska, with statehood, would promptly act to remove the fish traps from Alaska waters. In that fear they are undoubtedly correct. The people of Alaska, under the present system, are powerless to act.

"So we ask you to report this bill favorably. Statehood is Alaska's right and destiny. Alaska does not come before this committee as a supplicant. It asserts the ancient right of petition to the Congress of the United States. Our case is just and fortified with facts. The time for this committee, and for the Senate, to act affirmatively with respect to Alaska is now."

The C. I. O. sent Anthony W. Smith, at the request of President Philip Murray and General Counsel Arthur Goldberg, to present the support of that great labor organization, with six million members, of the pending statehood legislation.

He cited the resolution adopted by its national executive board the previous May which read, in part, as follows:

> "The citizens of Alaska, under the able stewardship of Governor Ernest Gruening, have demonstrated their devotion to Democratic principles and contributed mightily to the recent war effort.
>
> "The continued denial of full political democracy to the people of Alaska endangers the whole concept of a democratic society."

Father Paul C. O'Connor, S.J., of Hooper Bay, Alaska, said he had come further than any other witness, and had lived in Alaska for 20 years. I had appointed him Chairman of the Board of the Alaska Housing Authority. His testimony fascinated the Senators.

". . . . We are tired of waiting. We are capable of going ahead because we have maturity. We have more education, as much if not more than any State in the beginning of their statehood. . . . Of course, it will be hard sledding. What of it? In Alaska we thrive on difficulties. We are inured to them, but we surmount them. I have personally faced death a dozen times. I have been lost in a high wind on the Bering Sea in a small boat and was almost washed over to Siberia. I have actually gone down with a sled between the ice floes on the Yukon. I have wandered around the tundra in a blizzard for three solid days without food for myself or my dogs. To top it all, I fell into an overflow at the end of three days and was a cake of ice from the waist down. . . . You say the trials of statehood are of a different caliber. Let them come!'

W. O. Smith, fisherman of Ketchikan, a troller, discussed the adverse effects of fishtraps.

Lee Bettinger, serving his fourth term as Mayor of Kodiak, testified as to the difficulty of getting land on that island because of reservations made by various Federal agencies, protests against which proved unavailing.

The Reverend R. Rolland Armstrong, Presbyterian Minister representing his church's Board of Missions in Alaska, suggested that "not all decisions are based on economy, politics and pres--sure groups. Emotionally and morally, people need security. Statehood will give us a richer future and a stronger people."

He also cited the report of the National Home Missions Congress representing 24 Protestant denominations, meeting in the preceding January, that "recognizing that Territorial status permits discrimination and retards progress and local responsibility, we urge Congress to grant statehood to Alaska."

Essie R. Dale, of Fairbanks, Democratic National Committeewoman, testified that there were more college graduates in Fairbanks in proportion to population than in any other American city, and that in the plane chartered to bring Alaskans to the hearing, the fifty passengers had come to Alaska from thirty-seven states—illustrating what a cross-section of Americans constituted Alaska's population.

Other witnesses testifying for statehood were: Nick Sablick, of Anchorage, soda fountain owner and operator; John Ryan, engineer, of Anchorage; Howard Lyng, of Nome, miner and Democratic National Committeeman, born in Alaska in 1892 of Norwegian parents; John Hellenthal, lawyer, city attorney of Anchorage, likewise Alaskan-born; Don Goodman, president of the Anchorage Chamber of Commerce; Eleanor Jones, of Anchorage, housewife; Ruth Moore, Anchorage, secretary for the Department of Public Welfare; Gladys Grady, President of the Business and Professional Women's Club of Anchorage; Mrs. Doris McKinley, of Palmer, whose husband, Dr. Lee McKinley, was a candidate for the Territorial House of Representatives on the Republican ticket; Mrs. C. D. (Leslie) Wright, of Washington, D.C., who brought the support of the 5,500,000 members of the General Federation of Women's Clubs, which, she testified, had been on record for Alaskan statehood for the last six years; Russell Hermann, of Juneau, law school student. Mrs. Alfred Owen, of Anchorage, testified that her three sons had served in World War II and felt deprived at being unable, as Alaskans, to vote for President. Arthur (Al) Lintner, who served in the Aleutians as a G.I. and later as a Colonel at Anchorage during the war, added his word for statehood. Frank Haley, a veteran of the Spanish-American War and World War I testified for statehood in behalf of the Regular Veterans Association.

Frank Peratrovich, born in Klawock, and several times its Mayor, former President of the Territorial Senate, and President of the Alaska Native Brotherhood, spoke feelingly about the evils of fishtraps and the damage they caused to the fisheries and to the economy of the fishing communities.

Alfred E. Owen, Jr., Vice President of the Alaska Territorial Federation of Labor, and Secretary of the United Fishermen of Cook Inlet, A. F. of L., testified that between 75 and 80 per cent of the people of Alaska were wage earners and had supported all the measures preparing Alaska for statehood adopted by the 1949 legislature, of which he was a member.

Robert B. Atwood, editor and publisher of the Anchorage Times, reviewing Alaska's history, compared long range rule from Washington with long range rule under the Czars when Alaska was Russian-America. "Throughout the years Alaska has been mistreated," he said, and proceeded to document that statement verbally and with a specially prepared booklet entitled: "83 Years of Neglect," written by his wife, Evangeline Atwood.

Opening Thursday, the fourth day of the hearing, was W. C. Arnold, attorney, Managing Director of Alaska Salmon Industry, Inc., of Seattle, an office he had held for five years.

He testified at great length in opposition to Alaska's admission to statehood, his testimony, with the Senators' questioning, consuming both the morning and afternoon sessions and continuing through all of the fifth day's hearing. He buttressed his testimony with an impressive array of graphs, charts and maps.

He did not agree, he said, with the proponents of statehood that it would cure many of the Territory's ills. If a non-contiguous area were admitted, he asked: "What about Puerto Rico, the Virgin Islands, Guam and Antarctica?"

Granting that the people of Alaska voted for statehood—and they were far from unanimous—was it "in the national interest? Was it in the interest of all the people, not just those who live in Alaska?"

But it was against the provisions of H. R. 331 that Mr. Arnold directed his fire. "Under the bill Alaska would be a state in name only, for the Federal Government still would retain over 99 per cent of the land area with little or no prospect that its release to State control or State taxation would take place.[3] By the bill, Alaska would be relegated to the status of a mendicant State; a poor and distant relative, to so speak."

Mr. Arnold contended that this fact was not generally understood in Alaska as elsewhere, that H. R. 331 differed from H. R. 206

on which the extensive hearings had been held, in that H. R. 206 gave Alaska all the Federal Government's vacant and unappropriated land, so that in his "honest judgment. . . .knowingly or unknowingly, the advocates of the passage of H. R. 331, in their anxiety to reach their objectives," had "perpetrated a great hoax on the people of Alaska and of the Nation." [4]

"The public lands provisions to which I have referred are contained in sections 3, 4 and 5 of the bill. I have serious objections to these sections of the bill. H. R. 206, with a few exceptions, would transfer· to the new State title to the public lands located in Alaska. This is contrary to the traditional practice which has been followed throughout the West when new states have been admitted to the Union. The custom has been for the Federal Government to grant to the new States lands for schools and for internal improvements, but to retain the bulk of the public lands under Federal ownership. I strongly recommend that there be no change in this practice in the case of Alaska. The public lands in the Territory were purchased by the United States for the benefit of the Nation as a whole and are, in effect, held in trust for the people of the United States. Congress, as the ultimate manager of the property of all the people, should not turn it over to the relatively few who live in Alaska to use as a source of revenue. Not only would the people of the United States be deprived of their property, but also there would be no assurance that the land and its resources would be developed prudently or in accordance with national needs, nor that the land would be made available to settlers from the other States. Instead, it could be sold in large tracts to a few individuals in order to produce revenue for the State.

"In line with the preceding comments, I recommend the inclusion in H. R. 206 of provisions which would permit Alaska to enter into the Union on a basis similar to that on which the western continental States were admitted. While retaining the greater part of the public lands for national management the Federal Government has made grants to the new States for school purposes and internal improvements. Similar grants should be made in the case of Alaska.

"Specifically, I recommend grants which would allow Alaska over 21,000,000 acres for the support of its common schools, over 438,000 acres for the support of its agricultural college and school of mines, and 500,000 acres for other internal improvements. This is a far greater amount of public lands than any other State has been given upon its admission."

In consequence of the Interior Dept.'s opposition, H. R. 206 was never reported by the Subcommittee, and Delegate Bartlett introduced H. R. 331 in its stead.

Furthermore, Mr. Arnold said: "The bill, if enacted, would automatically and by operation of law subject every acre of land in the new State, whether State-owned, Federally owned, or privately owned, to the cloud of Indian title. The bill requires the people of Alaska, as a condition of statehood, to acknowledge existence of unextinguished Indian title to the very homes in which they live and to accept the State lands subject to unextinguished native rights, rights which the courts have held do not exist, rights previously not in existence but sought to be revived and recreated by this measure."

"Since only the Federal Government can settle the Indian claims," continued Mr. Arnold, "and since the Department of the Interior is continually advocating that they be settled in favor of the Indians or not at all, the prospect of State income from that source is not bright."

"I believe," he concluded, that "that clause, if enacted, would cast a cloud on practically all land titles within the proposed State. . . .and the new State will be dealt a death blow at the very moment of its birth."

Mr. Arnold also stressed the lack of surveys which would delay for a long time the acquisition by the new State of the four numbered sections.

Commenting on the rate at which the Department of the Interior had been making surveys, Senator Anderson calculated that it would require 17,000 years to complete Alaska's surveys.

On Friday, April 28th, Mr. Arnold introduced Rear Admiral Ralph Wood, retired, who, during World War II, had commanded the Seventeenth Naval District which comprised Alaska. Admiral Wood, Mr. Arnold stated, came to testify at his (Arnold's) request "and at the expense of the Alaska Salmon Industry, Inc."

Admiral Wood's testimony was to the effect that Alaska would be defended equally whether a Territory or a State, and was designed to refute previous testimony that statehood would strengthen the national defense.

Mr. Arnold then introduced Edward W. Allen, a Seattle attorney who had served as a Presidential appointee on various international fisheries commissions and whose law firm had also represented "substantial Alaska interests."

He raised the question of the desirability of changing the control of the fisheries to the State of Alaska because of their international aspects, and also questioned as ambiguous the language that povided such transfer in H.R. 331.

My testimony concluded the hearings. It covered aspects not before presented to the committees of Congress. In part it was devoted to refuting some of the objections to statehood and to bringing in some little known material from the history of other Territories' battles for statehood which I had researched and proved useful in comparison with Alaska of their populations and other circumstances surrounding their efforts to gain admission.

In response to a challenging request from Senator Eugene Milliken, R., of Colorado, to show how statehood for Alaska would "strengthen the Union," I developed what I believed to be the great benefits which Alaska's admission would bring to the whole United States. Senator Milliken was kind enough to say:

"If Governor Gruening were Senator from Alaska he could charm a bird out of a tree."

Finally, since the opposition was now not so much against statehood itself but against the bill, H. R. 331, I defended it as by no means as good a bill as we would like, but as the best bill Alaska could hope to obtain at that time, as demonstrated by the opposition both from the Federal bureaus and in the Congress to the more generous versions previously introduced by Delegate Bartlett. The provisions of H. R. 331 had been widely publicized in Alaska and met with widespread approval and preference for prompt action rather than delay in the hope of securing a better bill, such opposition as there was coming from those already on record as against statehood itself.

Immediately after the hearings, I called President Truman to report on the obviously favorable attitude of the committee and asked him to press for action at that concluding session of the 81st Congress. This he did in a letter to Senator O'Mahoney, the chairman of the committee, on May 5th. The Committee reported the bill on June 7th, with only the dissenting view of Senator Butler. The report gave the Committee's view that the bill, as amended, had the support of the great majority of Alaskans in all walks of life and that the burden of opposition "was carried by representatives of the fish packing industry with headquarters in the States;" that the bill, as amended, "would be the most generous enabling act under which any State ever came into the Union."

That was true. For the Committee had changed the House bill's provision of four numbered sections in each township to a free choice of a total of 21,400,000 acres of unreserved lands, including 200,000 acres from the National Forests.

So, with the Alaska and Hawaii statehood bills enacted by the House and reported by the Senate in June, and the strong support of the executive branch, the outlook for favorable action in the 81st Congress appeared promising. But eight years were to pass before Alaska's statehood was achieved.

The Korean War had begun and Senate action on the statehood bills languished. A motion on August 8th to bring them up on the consent calendar was objected to by Senator Pat McCarran, D., of Nevada, and they "went over". Similar motions on September 13th were blocked by the objection of Senator Walter F. George, D., of Georgia. The session recessed on September 23rd to permit the members running for re-election to campaign, and reconvened on November 27th. On that day, Vice-President Barkley laid before the Senate a letter from President Truman urging prompt approval of the Alaska and Hawaii bills.

The next day, on the motion by Majority Leader Scott Lucas, D., of Illinois, to proceed to the consideration of the Alaska bill, it was clear that its opponents would strive to delay and prevent action in the 81st Congress, the lateness of the season favoring their purpose. The motion to proceed was never agreed to. Nevertheless a three-day debate of substantial merit and eloquence took place. Those supporting statehood were: Joseph C. O'Mahoney, D., of Wyoming, floor manager of the bill; Anderson, D., of New Mexico; Lehman, D., of New York; Langer, R., of No. Dakota; Ecton, R., of Montana; Cordon, R., of Oregon; Aiken, R., of Vermont; Thye, R., of Minnesota; Morse, R., of Oregon. Those opposing were: Butler, R., of Nebraska; Stennis, D., of Mississippi; Eastland, D., of Mississippi; Russell, D., of Georgia; McClellan, D., of Arkansas; Hoey, D., of North Carolina; McKellar, D., of Tennessee.

As Governor I had access to the Senate floor and was able to furnish refutations to Senator Butler's deliberate misrepresentations as well as to the citations by other opponents as arguments against statehood of the very conditions in Alaska which we ascribed to our Territorial status and were contending that statehood would cure.

Alleging it to be "a physical impossibility" for the State of Alaska "to assume or to meet the financial responsibilities of statehood," Butler declared: "The budget has not been balanced. . . .They have enacted a number of tax laws, thinking they were going to raise a good part of the money which they were appropriating. . . .Without exception these laws have been declared unconstitutional by the local court."

The truth was that the 1949 legislature had balanced the budget, left unbalanced by the 1947 legislature, and that with one modification in the progressive fish trap tax, all the revenue measures —income tax, personal property tax, business license tax, permissive sales tax—enacted by it had been sustained by the courts.

Senator Cordon deplored the fact that statehood opponents had taken advantage of every parliamentary situation and had not permitted the bills to come up for a vote, concluding with an encouraging plea to continue trying.

After three days, given in part to the debate, on December 5th Senator Lucas, who had been defeated for re-election in November by Everett Dirksen, gave up and took up other "unfinished business". Statehood supporters felt he had given in too soon and too easily, although in retrospect it seems clear that with only three weeks remaining before the Christmas recess and adjournment, the filibuster could not have been overcome.

W HILE disappointed, we were not in the least discouraged. We had made important progress. We now had substantial volumes of hearing records presenting Alaska's case. For the first time Alaskan statehood had been debated on the Senate floor. Both houses of Congress had now laid the case for statehood before the country. While we were keenly aware that much remained to be done, that more public opinion needed to be mobilized, we were prepared and eager to do it. So, we girded ourselves for the next round.

In the 83rd Congress, the leadership properly decided that since the House had enacted statehood bills while the Senate had not, the Senate should now initiate the next try. Objectors prevented action during the first session, and the Alaska bill was not brought up till January 31, 1952. It was known that a coalition of "Taft Republicans" and Southern Democrats were planning to recommit the bill—that is, sending it back to committee—a well-established method of defeating a measure without actually voting against it and incurring whatever onus might attach to such a vote. After a spirited debate which consumed the greater part of eleven days over a period of four weeks, the bill was recommitted by the narrowest of margins, by a vote of 45 to 44, on February 27th, the issue remaining in doubt until the last vote was cast. It was an important step forward, despite its adverse result.

A few weeks before, Senator Kenneth Wherry, R., of Nebraska, had died and the State's Governor, Val Peterson, had appointed Fred A. Seaton, newspaper publisher and radio station owner, to the vacancy. Coming to Washington to be present at the debate, I called upon Senator Seaton with a view to "selling" him on statehood. He greeted me in most friendly fashion, saying: "I am wholly uninformed on the subject. But I'd be glad to be informed." I was in his office for two hours. Then he said: "I want to talk to Joe Farrington about Hawaii. Come back in a few days and I'll give you my answer."

I was not optimistic. The most inveterate opponent of statehood for both Alaska and Hawaii was Seaton's senior colleague from Nebraska, Hugh Butler. He had been the Chairman of the Public Lands (later Interior and Insular Affairs) Committee of the Senate in the 80th Congress. It seemed inevitable to me that Seaton would consult with Butler on this issue, and would bow to his seniority and recent experience with the subject in hand. Indeed, I was fully prepared to hear from Fred Seaton that while he was deeply sympathetic with our aspirations for statehood, that after all it was a new subject for him, and his senior colleague, who had given the matter much first-hand and intensive study, felt that Alaska was not ready, etc., etc., and that therefore he, Fred Seaton, would have, for the time being, to be opposed.

So, I was more than pleasantly surprised, a week later when I entered Fred Seaton's inner office in the Senate Office Building, to have him boom out at me:

"I've made up my mind. I'm for statehood now—for both Alaska and Hawaii."

I was delighted. Obviously desirous of more information, Seaton asked me to sit down and discuss the subject further.

I had, during the previous years, done intensive research on the struggle of each Territory to secure statehood. I had read the record of every debate in both houses of Congress, beginning with Vermont, the fourteenth State. I had learned many fascinating and little known facts that would stand us in good stead in our struggle. Perhaps the most interesting was Nebraska's story, whose admission to the Union, coincidentally, took place in 1867, the same year as the purchase of Alaska.

The amazing story here was that Nebraska had not fulfilled the requirements for admission to statehood; that the Senate hearings developed several instances of flagrant fraud in counting the votes supposedly cast for its admission, which were less than a majority, and that President Andrew Johnson had vetoed the Nebraska Statehood Bill for that reason. However, Johnson was at the height of his unpopularity in the Congress. He had escaped impeachment a few weeks earlier by the margin of one vote and so, with a mighty whoop, the House overrode the veto and Nebraska came into the Union.

In my testimony before the Senate Interior and Insular Affairs Committee on April 29, 1950, I had included this story in detail, as one illustration of a State coming in with far less justification than Alaska had, and I also detailed the somewhat different, but also pertinent, stories of Oregon and Wyoming. When I had finished, Senator Butler said: "It happened back before my time. I have no doubt it is absolutely the truth. . . It is very interesting."

Now, nearly two years later, I was telling the story of how his own State had gotten into the Union to another Nebraska Senator, Fred Seaton, who had never heard it. He was fascinated by it. He asked me to write it out in detail. In addition to presenting the facts about this and other earlier States, he accepted my suggestion that I draw the appropriate inferences. So, I wrote a speech which he delivered unchanged on the Senate floor on February 20th. Obviously, it was a strong pitch for statehood for Alaska and Hawaii. And it was the only speech that he delivered during his nearly thirteen months in the Senate, for he decided not to run for election and left the Senate at th expiration of the term on January 4, 1953. But there is a sequel which will follow shortly.

I should point out that there is nothing unusual in having someone draft a Senator's or a Congressman's speech for him. When he approves it, with or without alterations, it becomes his, and in this case Senator Seaton found it obviously useful to utilize his own State's almost unknown vicissitudes in achieving statehood in their bearing on the allegations of the inadequacy of Alaska's claims to statehood. He was warmly congratulated on his maiden speech by Senator McFarland and Senator O'Mahoney, who obviously welcomed his support.

In the 1952 elections, Dwight D. Eisenhower was elected President of the United States. Regardless of party, his election was hailed has a boon by statehood advocates, for two years previously, as President of Columbia University, speaking at Denver, he was reported by the Denver Post as follows:

> "Quick admission of Alaska and Hawaii to statehood will show the world that 'America practices what it preaches', General Dwight D. Eisenhower said Saturday in a brief talk to 1,500 Denverites gathered at the freedom bell.
> The famed war and peacetime leader declared admission of the two territories is 'in conformity with the American way of life', granting them self-government and equal voice in national affairs.
> "Alaskan and Hawaiian statehood will serve to the people of the world as a 'practical symbol that America practices what it preaches', Eisenhower said. He said he hopes Congress could soon pass admission legislation now before it." [2]

It came therefore as an unpleasant surprise and shock to Alaskans when, in his State of the Union Message on February 2, 1953, President Eisenhower endorsed statehood for Hawaii but omitted any mention of Alaska. Furthermore, he urged that Hawaii be granted statehood "promptly with the first election scheduled for 1954."

The emphasis on the 1954 election indicated that the President had been apprised of the desirability of increasing, at the first opportunity, the Republican hair-breadth majority in the Senate. Henceforth, as indeed for several years previously, the assumption that Hawaii would elect Republicans and Alaska Democrats would play an important part in Congressional maneuverings on statehood for the two Territories.

The Alaska legislature, which had assembled in Juneau less than a week earlier, was heavily Republican as a result of the previous November landslide. Its legislators immediately wired President Eisenhower, protesting Alaska's omission, and followed it up with a memorial adopted by the unanimous votes of both houses, requesting consideration of Alaskan statehood similar to Hawaii's.

But no change in attitude was forthcoming from the White House. President Eisenhower explained his new stand by voicing his belief that Alaska was not ready for it. But his reversal, generally attributed to political motivations, strengthened state-hood sentiment in Alaska.

I had retired from the governorship on April 10, 1953, to be succeeded by President Eisenhower's appointee, B. Frank Heintzle-man, who had not been a supporter of statehood. I started work immediately on a book which I hoped, by a presentation of the historical interaction of political and economic factors, would, for the first time, afford understanding of Alaska's need for self-government. "The State of Alaska", 606 pages in length, ap-peared in the fall of 1954. It was to prove a helpful reference book to the statehood cause. I sought to keep it as objective as possible, allowing the facts to speak for themselves, as I believe they did.

In the Senate, the Republican majority on the Committee on Interior and Insular Affairs decided to report the Hawaii bill, S. 49, but not the Alaska Bill, S. 50. To obviate this discrimina-tion, Senator Anderson moved that the bills be joined and hear-ings ordered on both.

Hearings were held in Alaska in the summer of 1953. Senator Butler did his best to prevent their taking place, but when he found that Interior Committee members were determined to go, whether he did or not, he went. The others were: Frank A: Barrett, R., of Wyoming; James E. Murray, D., of Montana; Clinton P. Anderson, D., of New Mexico; Earle C. Clements, D., of Kentucky; and Henry M. Jackson, D., of Washington. Bob Bartlett accompanied them.

Hearings began in Ketchikan on August 17th. Senator Butler had announced that he wanted to hear from the "little people" of Alaska. Lester Gore, attorney, presented as in line with his views an editorial by Sid Charles in the Ketchikan News, which began:

> "We're against statehood for Alaska at the present time. . . .
> Statehood at this time would mean far too heavy a tax burden
> without corresponding benefits. . . .Rather than statehood now, with
> its additional burdens, would it not be far better to enlist the aid
> of the present Republican administration for removal of antiquated,
> conflicting, frustrating, and overlapping bureau regulations in order
> to invite and encourage development of our resources with the re-
> sults of a permanent and stable population and economy."

Testifying for statehood were: Douglas S. Smith, a timber cruiser; Mrs. L. L. Olsen, a fisherman's wife, who said that the fishermen's wives were unanimously for statehood; Charles I. Rice, operating engineer, who was concerned that the State should control the natural resources; Walter T. Stuart, consulting engi-neer, and Vice President of the Board of Regents of the Uni-versity of Alaska; the Reverend Wyburn Skidmore, Methodist minister, who felt that Senator Butler's bill for an elective Gov-ernor was "simply a sop thrown at us. . . .which would hold statehood back 10 or 15 years." He noted that "by and large, the proponents of statehood are among those who are in the lower-income bracket, and the opponents of statehood primarily are those of larger industry and larger holdings." Mrs. Margaret Ellis, who pointed out that her great grandfather left Germany to escape taxation and conscription without representation, that his son had volunteered for service in the Union Army, and that her husband and son were volunteers in the United States military service, but that they lacked the representation that all Americans were entitled to; Chris Bakkem, a fisherman, who saw fishing going down every year; Harry Cowah, who was highly critical of the Fish and Wildlife Service's management of the fisheries; Eugene Wacker, of Wacker, 56 years a resident, who said: "If you allow us to paddle our canoe, if we become a State, we will overcome all of these obstacles that you are speaking about."; Carl J. Foss, construction engineer, who, along with statehood, recommended "a sharp curtailment of the multitudinous Federal bureaus" and "in order to foster at an early date a homogeneous State, the Indian Bureau should be eliminated, and the natives assimilated into the citizenry."

At Juneau, and on the rest of the tour, on August 15th, an interested listener was Riley H. Allen, editor of the Honolulu Star-Bulletin. Witnesses testifying for statehood were the Reverend Fred McGinnis, Assistant Superintendent of Methodist Work in Alaska; Dr. William Whitehead, physician; Carl W. Heinmiller, of Haines, who was critical of "the old aristocracy of Alaska who are against statehood because they don't want to pay their share."; Peter Wood, realtor; Jack McFarland, editor of the local weekly newspaper; Jane McMullen, housewife with four children; Dorothy Whitney, Public Health nurse; Fred Soberg, fisherman; Jack Doyle, former Assistant to the Governor; Jasper Heath, who complained of the difficulty of getting land from the Bureau of Land Management; Kenneth J. Kadow, President of the United States Tin Corporation, and formerly head of the Alaska Field Committee as Representative of the Secretary of the Interior, who said:

> ". . . .Alaska will never move forward as fast and as well as it can until it gets in a position where many of the basic courses of economic and social direction are clearly within its own hands. In the capacity with the Interior Department that I enjoyed up here, my job boiled down primarily to being an expediter. The job had many other ramifications, but at least 90 per cent of my time was spent in trying to make bureaucracy get out of the way. Everybody knows that practically all the resources, and practically all of the land, the minerals, and everything else that we call Alaska is under the control of the Federal Government.
>
> "Whenever you try to work on any phase of the public domain, you run smack dab into the Federal Government.
>
> "There is no substitute in any way, shape, or form, for dealing with the Federal Government than through your elected representatives. These. . . .in order to be really effective must be or should be at least the caliber of a Senator. . . .
>
> "Under the. . . .guidance of Secretary Ickes, Alaska was under wraps. You practically could do nothing because there was no phase of the public domain that interested the Secretary as a development feature. While that administration lasted, Alaska stagnated."

Speaking in opposition to statehood were: R. J. Sommers, President of R. J. Sommers Construction Co., who felt the current economy would not support statehood; Robert Druxman, realtor, who felt the pending statehood bill was entirely unsatisfactory; Mrs. Myrth B. Sarvela, of Sitka, Secretary, Northern Fishing Owner Association, who introduced extensive correspondence with Fish and Wildlife officials urging compliance with a legislative memorial that herring be not taken for reduction. The response was negative and unsatisfactory to Mrs. Sarvela. Senator Anderson sought vainly to find out why Mrs. Sarvela wanted no change from the existing system to statehood.

Marcus Jensen, of Douglas, a Territorial Senator, said he was "definitely for statehood when I feel we can afford it. . . .I couldn't vote for statehood at this time."

Allen Shattuck, owner of an insurance agency in Juneau and a past Territorial legislator, presented a written statement elaborating on his view "that the additional costs to be assumed to administer a State cannot be raised without putting such a heavy tax burden upon our people that it will do two things: first, discourage new capital and, second, drive both people and invested capital out."

A letter from Mrs. Nina Crumrine and her daughter, Josephine Crumrine, well-known artists, living in Haines, was introduced by Senator Butler, saying: "The Territory of Alaska is not ready for statehood due to its thin population. The actual taxpayers of Alaska are few in number when the irresponsible native population is counted out. . . .The boom in the interior has resulted entirely from the defense program and will die out when construction work is ended. Strategically, Alaska is impossible to hold in case of attack."

Frank Marshall, union representative for the Brotherhood of Carpenters, disagreed with an earlier statement that "most of the persons. . . .interested in statehood were young. A lot of us grew old waiting for statehood. I have been 25 years. The Labor movement in Alaska had been striving for statehood," he said.

Cledamae Cammock, Executive Secretary of the Alaska Territorial Federation of Labor, said that she had heard that it was the desire of the Senators "to hear the opinions of the little men. If there are any more or greater little men than the man who works as a laborer, who goes out and digs the ditches, the teamster who drives the trucks, the cab driver who transports citizens, visitors of Alaska, then I would like to see them."

Roger Hurlock, whose family consisted of a wife and six boys, and had established a poultry farm ten miles north of Juneau, was for statehood for both "practical" and "moral" reasons.

Warren Christiansen, attorney from Sitka, also President of the Sitka Chamber of Commerce, raised the problems of an inadequate judicial system under Territorial status and the need for proper mental health legislation which, for Alaska, depended on Congressional action.

Three more views from Sitka were introduced in the record.

Leslie Yaw, Presbyterian missionary, and Joe H. Ashby, writing for the Sitka Chamber of Commerce, endorsed the pending statehood bill. Harold and Ernestine Veatch, owners and editors of the Daily Sitka Sentinel, felt that a state composed of the First Division and all but the western part of the Third would be justifiable, but that the rest of the Territory, sparsely settled, should be excluded.

On the second day's hearing in Juneau, Norman Banfield, attorney, entered into an interesting discussion with the committee members on the education of the Natives and on the problems involved in creating counties.

Favoring statehood were Mrs. Sandra Zenger, housewife; Belle Simpson, owner of The Nugget Shop; Ralph Browne, who gave an extensive account of Alaskan resource potentials; Fred Hanford, Wrangell businessman, who recalled that he had introduced the first pro-statehood memorial in the 1945 legislature, and that while statehood was past due, it seemed a little farther away than it had been because the 1953 legislature repealed the Property Tax Act enacted by the 1949 legislature, which he felt should have been retained.

A statement by Burke Riley, Secretary of Alaska, was directed at refuting the opposition's cry: "Now is not the time." "Alaskans," he pointed out, "have fought in four wars, yet are still denied full membership in the Union," adding: "Show us a State that was subjected to a longer qualifying period, to greater indignities, to more pointed discriminations. Show us a State better prepared on admission than is Alaska today—a State with fewer initial liabilities, or with greater initial promise."

From Petersburg, Bernice and Ragnar Stokke, owners of the Arctic Hotel, expressed their support of statehood.

B. D. Stewart, mining engineer, former Mayor of Juneau, and former Territorial Commissioner of Mines, gave as "the considered opinion of a life here of over 43 years" that statehood was overdue.

Following him, his son, Thomas B. Stewart, one of the two Assistant Attorney-Generals of the Territory, gave a detailed and spirited account of various discriminations suffered as a result of Territorial status. He pointed to, as disgraceful, that there had been no Federal judge in Anchorage since May 28th, and that the Second Judicial Division had been without a judge for nearly a year and without a District Attorney for 8 months. As a result of this Federal failure, many people were unable to go to court. He pointed to the differences in the Senate reports on statehood when, in 1951, Senator Butler was not Chairman of the Interior Committee.

Territorial Senator Elton Engstrom called attention to the inability of the fishermen to get the relief they had repeatedly requested from Congress through legislative memorials to abolish fishtraps and to stop the fishing for herring for reduction plants.

Other pro-statehood witnesses were: Dorothy Smith Gruening, housewife; Jerry Wade, currently a student at Notre Dame; Eldon

L. Taylor, meat cutter, and Commander of Taku Post, Veterans of Foreign Wars, who stated that its more than 200 members had voted unanimously for years for statehood; and Thomas A. Morgan, President of the Columbia Lumber Company, the Tongass Timber Corporation, and the Juneau Lumber Company, who pointed out that his activities had taken him to every part of Alaska.

In Fairbanks, on August 20th, Dick Swain, business agent for the plasterers and cement workers and a homesteader at Homer, discussed the difficulties in getting credit, and pointed out that employment was necessary for the homesteader to succeed.

Witnesses supporting statehood were: Ralph J. Rivers, Mayor of Fairbanks; Stanley Tatom, a machinery distributor, President of Yukon Equipment Company; Paul Solka, Jr., owner of Pioneer Printers; Cecil M. Wells, President of Wells Alaskan Motors, a General Motors car and truck agency; Hubert Gilbert, attorney; Richard J. Greuel, Territorial legislator and program director for Station K.F.A.R.; Andrew Nerland, businessman and former Territorial legislator; John Brennan, who agreed with Senator Anderson that the tourist possibilities of Alaska were tremendous and not yet touched and, with others, was developing a resort at Chena Hot Springs; J. A. Boulet, public accountant, who testified that he, his wife, and two fine healthy children were "real happy" in Alaska but were thinking of leaving if statehood did not come; the Reverend Victor Alfsen, Presbyterian minister; Mike Stepovich, attorney and Territorial Senator; Niilo Koponen, homesteader and worker on the line crew at the Fairbanks Exploration Company; James Ryan, former Commissioner of Education of Alaska and Superintendent of Schools for the Fairbanks Independent School District. Mr. Ryan said:

> "We have developed a school system in Alaska, a Territorial school system, without one single cent of Federal assistance, that is second to none. I realize that you will discount that somewhat because of my profession and because I have had some small part in that development, but we are indeed very proud of our school system. In fact, I would go so far as to say I believe. . . .our public school systems and parochial school systems are superior to those of many States which have been States for many years. We are told that if we expect the rights and privileges of statehood, we must at the same time assume the responsibilities, and I would like to turn it around to say that if we have assumed those responsibilities, then we, as American citizens, have the right to claim the privileges and the rights of citizens."

William E. Beltz, of Nome, Eskimo, who had served one term in the Territorial House of Representatives and two in the Senate, replying to a question as to whether decisions in Washington were made by people who do not understand Alaska's local problems, replied: "Precisely, yes." To which the questioner, Senator Clements, replied: "I want heartily to agree with that statement because. . . .even in the few days I have been in Alaska I have a little different conception of your problems than I had last week."

Herbert W. Hamilton, Director of Education for the on-base schools in northern Alaska, favoring statehood, supported Mr. Ryan's views as to the high quality of education in Alaska, saying that students coming from the States "are necessarily put back a grade to compete with children here in Fairbanks."

Lee S. Gardner voiced his belief that wildlife resources would be much better handled by the State.

Jerry Adams, student at the University of Alaska, asked how the majority of those young people felt about statehood, replied:

> "I can explain that by saying that we have a student paper that comes out weekly, and we had one editor at the first of the year who opposed statehood. He is now an ex-editor of the paper, and he was after the first edition."

Supporting statehood also were: Robert J. McNealy, attorney; Harry B. Avakoff, jewelry store owner; Stan Caulfield, printer; Everett Patton, engaged in the tourist business.

In opposition were: Mike Erceg, operating and consulting drill expert, who declared:

> "I am against statehood for Alaska for the reason we can't support it. . . .Our gold mining, copper, lead, zinc and all mining industries are down 80 per cent from the last war. High cost of living has gone up. Prices on metals mined are way down. Transportation to Alaska is too high. On Alaska fisheries, it costs too much to catch and can them and they can't sell it. . . ."

Mr. Erceg presented several pages from the Fairbanks News-Miner which showed the delinquent property tax rolls for several past years. Senator Butler inserted them in the record of the hearings, where they occupied 15 pages.

Mrs. Charles Canfield, certified public accountant, declared: "I don't think we are ready for statehood. I don't think we can afford it."

Mrs. Alyce Stuart felt there should be another referendum on statehood, and that the question should be worded "immediate statehood".

Julian A. Hurley, attorney, said:

> "I have lived in Alaska for more than 31 years. And I appear here as one of the original opponents of statehood. Another old-line Democrat and I, an old-line Republican, appeared on a public hearing before the question was submitted to the voters of Alaska, in a debate that was broadcast, and we opposed statehood at that time. . . Many of the objections I have to statehood at the present time are the same as they were then. . . .When the United States purchased Alaska from Russia by that very act of purchase they assumed a certain obligation, and that obligation was to develop the Territory of Alaska. Not only that, in Alaska there were a certain number of natives and they assumed the obligation of looking after the natives.
>
> "Since that time, the Federal Government has failed, not only in the obligation they assumed, but they have failed to take care of the natives and they have forced it on the people of the Territory of Alaska. I want to say freely and frankly, the people of Alaska did not purchase Alaska. It was purchased by the United States.

So it went along and I had hopes. When I came out against state-hood, I had hopes that the Federal Government would perform its full duty under the obligation incurred to the Territory of Alaska, and they never have."

Later in his testimony, Mr. Hurley said:

"Personally, I was opposed to statehood because I did not think we were ready for it. But the only way we can fight the Socialists in the Department of the Interior and the rest of the gang against the individual ownership of property, is to get statehood and get a couple of Senators back in Washington to fight for Alaska. I am sorry that that has to be done but if they would give us what we are entitled to, I wouldn't be in favor of statehood at the present time. But I have watched this thing for years, and I see no other chance in the world for Alaska to get what it is entitled to, unless we get somebody back in the United States Senate to fight . . . and get what we are entitled to."

At Anchorage, on August 24th, A. G. Hiebert, in the business of radio broadcasting and President of the Anchorage Chamber of Commerce, which had repeatedly endorsed statehood, testified at length on Anchorage's potentials, saying:—

"It is now more evident than ever before that Alaska will not come into its place in the sun until various departments of the Federal Government relinquish or surrender some of the life and death powers they hold over Alaska's economic development. . . .

"In the Matanuska Valley are coal deposits which industry wants to develop but they are tied up in reserves. Deposits of strategic and critical minerals remain undeveloped while government purchase contracts for hundreds of millions of dollars are granted companies operating in the wilds of Canada, Africa and South America. Tourist lodges do not go up in the national forests and elsewhere because the best sites usually are located on withdrawn land, or the leases and regulations governing their use are so stringent and limited that investment money cannot be obtained.

"The preceding are but a few of the manmade problems confronting development. We feel that many of these obstacles can be overcome by granting Alaska statehood now."

Victor Fischer, Anchorage City Planning Director, introduced tables and spoke on past and prospective city growth.

John E. Croul, Jr., Manager of the Anchorage Chamber of Commerce, discussed employment statistics and prospects.

Walter J. Hickel, hotel operator and contractor, testified that "as a Territory we are in a helpless situation regarding our lands . . . as a Territory we are stagnant; therefore it is obvious that as a State we could not go anywhere but forward."

Elmer Rasmuson appeared both as a representative of the Anchorage Republican Club, which by unanimous vote had endorsed immediate statehood, and in his own behalf as an Alaskan-born resident and banker.

"Statehood", he said, "would be a change, and I strongly advocate this change because of the benefits which cannot come in any other way. These benefits are two-way—for Alaska and for the Nation. These two-way benefits are also of two kinds—economic and social.

"Taking up the economic development of Alaska itself, we are presently a land of shackles. We have restrictive land laws which are an absurdity. Our Organic Act is obsolete. We are restricted in control of our major industries, namely, fishing. We are excluded from the Federal Highway Aid Act. The Jones Act restricts our shipping. Our wild game, with all its tourist potentialities, is out of our control. We cannot settle the Indian claims problem. We have no power to coordinate military spending to facilitate economic development. These restrictions can be removed automatically by the substitution of statehood."

Harry B. Palmer, engineer, spoke on the power needs of the Greater Anchorage area.

Alfred Owen, a member of the Anchorage Port Commission, spoke of port and transportation development.

E. Bradford Phillips, Alaskan manager of the Arctic Travel Service, spoke of the tourist industry.

George R. Jones, accountant, discussed the increased costs of statehood, which, he concluded, "will not be burdensome nor excessive."

William H. Olsen, attorney, born and reared in Alaska, declared that while in the past an outspoken critic of statehood, he now favored "statehood now".

Mrs. Edwin B. Crittenden, wife of the well-known Anchorage architect, felt that it might be more impressive to have the committee learn not what Alaskans are saying, but what they were doing, and proceeded to list varied individual accomplishments illustrating initiative, imagination, public spirit and vision, as well as material success.

Dr. James E. O'Malley, physician and surgeon, described the medieval and barbaric method of treating Alaska's mentally disturbed. Under this archaic procedure, individuals suspected of mental illness were arrested, charged with the crime of being insane, tried by a jury of six with no competence to decide the issue, and if found "guilty", sent to jail or to the Morningside Sanitarium in Portland, Oregon. Alaskans had tried vainly since 1912 to change this.

Dr. Charles Anderson, Psychiatrist, of the Department of Health, confirmed Dr. O'Malley's horror story. "I came here for the first time in June of 1952", said Dr. Anderson, "and words failed to describe how shocked I was when I found that the mentally ill were confined to an evil jail. . . . Now you wonder why we feel we should talk about this in a hearing for statehood. . . . The Organic Act of Alaska specifically reserves to the Federal Government the care of the mentally ill. So the territory of Alaska can do nothing about it no matter how much they wish to."

John Uttersham, real estate broker, told of the difficulty individuals had getting a small piece of land—most of it was tied up in Federal reservations.

George Shannon, Anchorage City Manager, described the impediments in Alaska's Organic Act to achieving desirable home rule for Alaska's municipalities.

Maynard Taylor, Mayor of Anchorage, reported the unanimous endorsement of statehood by the City Council.

Joseph R. Walsh, Commander, Denali Post, Veterans of Foreign Wars, reported that at the Department of Alaska at Kodiak, on June 3, 1953, a resolution for immediate statehood was adopted unanimously.

Al McCuen, an Alaska Railroad employe, the next witness, said: "I have a small petition here. It is small because it is the work of one man and I am not organized as apparently the rest of the people are. Anyway, it says here:

"'We the undersigned are not in favor of statehood until such time as the population and development of industry warrants same. We feel this is far from the case at the present time.'"

Mr. McCuen then amplified the reasons for his position.

Herald Stringer, attorney, Territorial legislator, and former Department Commander of the American Legion, urged that statehood be granted Alaska at the next session of Congress. He cited Secretary of the Interior McKay's statements in favor of statehood for Hawaii as no less applicable to Alaska.

Mitchel Abood said he represented the little man, differing from Mr. McCuen, and submitted "the names of 3,129 little men throughout Alaska, on record as favoring statehood."

Mrs. Margaret Rutledge, Secretary-Controller of Reeve-Aleutian Airways and Republican National Committeewoman, spoke of the humiliation she felt when, as a result of the McCarran Act, she, like other Alaskans, were obliged to be cleared at the Sea-Tac Air Terminal. "Had Alaska had two Senators when the McCarran bill was considered", she said, "Alaskans would have been spared this indignity."[3]

Other witnesses for statehood were: J. Earl Cooper, attorney and former Judge; Barbara Dimmock, member of the Territorial House of Representatives; John Gorsuch, factory representative; Mrs. Paul Clumpner, President of the Anchorage Women's Club; Ken C. Johnson, insurance broker; Dorothy Prior, accountant; Millard Fillmore Alewine, representing the Alaska Territorial Federation of Labor; Mrs. William McSmith, real estate broker, and Executive Secretary of the National Association for the Advancement of Colored People in Alaska.

Larry Nelson began: "I am one of the little men sitting here in the audience. I came to the Territory in 1940 with $75 in my pocket. I look around me and I see many faces of other little men who came up here under the same circumstances. Am I right, fellows and ladies?", at which there was wild applause from the audience.

Wendell P. Kay, attorney, stated his "firm conviction that the great majority of Alaskans want statehood and want it now; that Alaska is ready for statehood, historically, politically, morally, economically, and every other way . . . and we will not see the full development of Alaska until we achieve statehood."

William A. Egan, Territorial Senator, who described himself as "a small businessman in the town of Valdez", recalled that in 1946 the question was put to the people of Alaska whether they wanted the abolition of fish traps; that they voted 10 to 1 for abolition but that nothing happened, because the fisheries were under Federal control, and so, this great resource—the salmon fishery—was impaired.

The second day's hearing at Anchorage opened with the insertion in the record by the Chairman of a letter from Jay S. Hammond, of King Salmon, in opposition to statehood, and congratulating Senator Butler for his awareness of the above outlined arguments.

Pro-statehood witnesses were: Edwin M. Suddock, who felt that statehood would unite Alaskans and diminish sectionalism; Ed Baldwin, co-owner and manager of the Alaska Seed Company, who spoke on agriculture's potentials.

Victor Rivers, engineer and former Territorial Senator, depicted the forces fighting statehood, which he felt controlled the appointment of the present Governor and of the Director of Territories—tracing that opposition to the $60 million dollars worth of trap-caught fish, mostly absentee-owned. Since it was probable that under statehood the traps would be abolished, the origin of the opposition to statehood and its ramifications became clear.

Other pro-statehood witnesses were: Mrs. Justine Parks, of Chugiak, President of the Alaska Rural Electric Cooperative Associations; E. G. Bailey, of Mountain View, trailer court operator; Jim Norene, relator, of Mountain View; Milo Fritz, M.D.; Ira Rothwell, of Cordova, member of the Territorial Fisheries Board who pictured the distressed condition of the salmon fishery under Federal mismanagement, saying:

> "There is no one else responsible for this but the United States Congress and those people they authorize to take care of this vast industry. We hold that you have practically, through your organizations, depleted this industry. Despite its depleted state, and before it is completely destroyed, turn it over to us and let us rebuild it. That is what we want through statehood."

After further hearings in Washington, the Senate floor debate in the Second Session of the 83rd Congress on the two bills, again numbered S. 49 and S. 50, lasted from March 4th to April 1, 1954. Then the Senate, under the able floor leadership of Senator Clinton Anderson, who told me in advance exactly what the count would be, by a vote of 57 to 28 approved the combined bills. The more than two-to-one majority was gratifying, but our pleasure was tempered by awareness that a part of that majority came from those who felt that there was a better chance to defeat the joint bills, and were counting on the House to do it.

Indeed, the House, under pressure from the Eisenhower administration to report only a Hawaii and not an Alaska bill, failed to act. So, the 83rd Congress came and went without the enactment of statehood legislation.

The same lack of result was repeated in the 84th Congress (1955-1957) where joint bills were reported early in the first session, S. 49 in the Senate by Senator James E. Murray, D., of Montana, on his behalf and fifteen co-sponsors.

In the House, H. R. 2535 was reported by Clair Engle on March 3rd—the first time a joint statehood bill had been reported by a House committee. It was, however, recommitted on May 10th on a motion by Representative John R. Pillion, R., of New York, by a vote of 218 to 170. It was a gloomy day for statehood's prospects.

VI

B UT meanwhile, events were shaping on the home front in Alaska that were destined to break the Congressional blockade of statehood legislation.

The 1955 legislature assembling in the Territorial capital, Juneau, on January 14, 1955, provided for a constitutional convention that would draft a constitution for the State that Alaskans hoped to bring into being, and appropriated $300,000 for its expenses.

The bill, House Bill No. 1, was introduced on the second day. It was accompanied by a House Joint Memorial which, under suspension of the rules, was passed by a vote of 22 to 0 (2 members absent) and ordered enrolled and engrossed on the same day. Reflecting the growing impatience of Alaskans at the administrative and resulting Congressional obstructionism, the 1955 legislature was in dead earnest in seeking statehood.

It passed the bill by a vote of 23 to 1 in the House and by a unanimous vote of all 16 Senators.[1]

The election was held on September 13, 1955. The 55 chosen delegates assembled at the University of Alaska on November 9th.[2]

I delivered the keynote address on the second day, entitled: "Let Us End American Colonialism."

In addition to drafting what political scientists declared to be "one of the best, if not the best, state constitutions ever written," the convention took another step of far-reaching consequence which its proponents and delegates had not anticipated. It arose from an inspired recommendation made by a public-spirited New Orleans businessman, George H. Lehleitner.

In researching American history, he discovered that a number of territories had departed from the conventional procedures for seeking admission to the Union as states.

The first of these was an area lying West of the Carolinas. Its people, envious that the area immediately to the North—Kentucky—had achieved statehood in 1792, and displeased that none of the first three Congresses had taken similar steps to bring in a prospective State which, for awhile, bore the name "Franklin", called a Constitutional Convention, drafted a Constitution, and elected two "Senators". This was easier then than later, as the popular election of Senators did not come until 1913 with the Seventeenth Amendment to the Constitution. The Territorial Legislature of Tennessee, in 1796, sent the two Senators to the national capital—then Philadelphia—who, four months later, brought back statehood.

Similar procedure was followed by Michigan in 1835; by Iowa in 1846; by California in 1850; by Minnesota in 1858; by Oregon in 1859; and by Kansas in 1861. But few Americans knew this intriguing bit of history.

Lehleitner served in the Navy in the Second World War and was stationed in the Hawaiian Islands. Aware of that Territory's aspiration for statehood and sympathetic with it, he proposed the adoption of this procedure.

But Joseph Rider Farrington, Hawaii's Delegate in Congress, and his predecessor, Samuel Wilder King, leaders in Hawaii's struggle for statehood, felt it unnecessary; they were expecting statehood without it. They were counting on President Eisenhower and Speaker Joseph W. Martin. Hawaii, too, had called a Constitutional Convention, and its people had ratified a proposed State Constitution on November 7, 1950. But that document had been gathering dust and had contributed nothing to promote Hawaii's statehood. Lehleitner feared that Alaska's constitution would meet the same consignment to oblivion.

Lehleitner had been suggesting to me and others that Alaska adopt a "Tennessee Plan". I thought it was a grand idea and urged him to present it to the Constitutional Convention with a number of whose delegates I discussed what I felt would be its benefits. Lehleitner accepted their invitation to present the case and they approved it. They provided that at the Territorial primary election to be held on April 24, 1956, when the proposed constitution would be submitted to the Alaskan electorate for approval or rejection, the people could also vote whether they wished to adopt what was now called the "Alaska-Tennessee Plan". If they did so, two Senators and a Representative from Alaska would be chosen at the Territory's 1956 General Election.

Party conventions nominated their candidates. At the election, William A. Egan and I were elected Senators and Ralph J. Rivers as Representative. Bob Bartlett chose to remain as Delegate. The three of us proceeded to Washington to be present at the opening session of the 85th Congress on January 7, 1957. We were not admitted to the floor of the Senate, as had been done in the case of Tennessee. Instead, we were promptly told by the Republican leadership that we would have to agree to run again if statehood were achieved. This seemed reasonable and proper; we naturally assented and the pending statehood bills so provided.

The 23rd Territorial legislature, meeting in March of 1957, had authorized a budget of $185,925.41 for the two years in which it was hoped we would produce the desired statehood legislation.

Prior to that, and right after the Constitutional Convention, the Statehood Committee authorized the printing of 7,500 copies of my Keynote Address in pamphlet form and charged me with the pleasant duty of distributing it where it might do the most good. From my Washington office, copies with accompanying letters went to journalists, political scientists, industry executives, and, of course, to every Member of Congress. They produced a gratifying response; more and more influential people were being enlisted in our statehood cause. The supply of pamphlets ran out early and,

ALASKA, WE ARE HERE !

Cartoonist D. R. Fitzpatrick of the St. Louis *Post-Dispatch* pictures the Alaska-Tennessee Plan delegation, which, after arriving in Washington, was not given the privileges of the floor of the Senate.

as they have become "collector's items", it seems appropriate to reprint the address here:

LET US END AMERICAN COLONIALISM

We meet to validate the most basic of American principles, the principle of "government by consent of the governed." We take this historic step because the people of Alaska who elected you, have come to see that their long standing and unceasing protests against the restrictions, discriminations and exclusions to which we are subject have been unheeded by the colonialism that has ruled Alaska for 88 years. The people of Alaska have never ceased to object to these impositions even though they may not have realized that such were part and parcel of their colonial status. Indeed the full realization that Alaska is a colony may not yet have come to many Alaskans, nor may it be even faintly appreciated by those in power who perpetuate our colonial servitude.

Half a century ago, a governor of Alaska, John Green Brady, contemplating the vain efforts of Alaskans for nearly forty years to secure even a modicum of workable self-government, declared:

"We are graduates of the school of patience."

Since that time Alaskans have continued to take post-graduate courses. Today, in 1955, sorely tried through 88 years of step-childhood, and matured to step-adulthood, Alaskans have come to the time when patience has ceased to be a virtue. But our faith in American institutions, our reverence for American traditions, are not only undimmed but intensified by our continuing deprivation of them. Our cause is not merely Alaskans'; it is the cause of all Americans. So we are gathered here, following action by our elected representatives who provided this Constitutional Convention, to do *our* part to "show the world that America practices what it preaches."*

These words are not original with me. But they remain as valued and as valid as when they were uttered five years ago. They remain no less valid even if their noble purpose is as yet unfulfilled. We are here to do what lies within our power to hasten their fulfillment.

We meet in a time singularly appropriate. Not that there is ever a greater or lesser timeliness for the application by Americans of American principles. Those principles are as enduring and as eternally timely as the Golden Rule. Indeed democracy is nothing less than the application of the Golden Rule to the Great Society. I mean, of course, democracy of deeds, not of lip-service; democracy that is faithful to its professions; democracy that matches its pledges with its performance. But there is nevertheless, a peculiar timeliness to this Alaskans' enterprise to keep our nation's democracy true to its ideals. For right now that the United States has assumed world leadership, it has shown through the expressions of its leaders its distaste for colonialism. And this antipathy to colonialism—wherever such colonialism may be found—reflects a deep-seated sentiment among Americans.

For our nation was born of revolt against colonialism. Our charters of liberty—the Declaration of Independence and the Constitution—embody America's opposition to colonialism and to colonialism's inevitable abuses. It is therefore natural and proper that American leadership should set its face against the absenteeism, the discriminations and the oppressions of colonialism. It is natural and proper that American leadership should lend such aid and comfort as it may to other peoples striving for self-determination and for that universally applicable tenet of American faith—government by consent of the governed. Indeed, as we shall see, we are pledged to do this by recent treaty commitments.

What more ironical, then, what more paradoxical, than that very very same leadership maintains Alaska as a colony?

What could be more destructive of American purpose in the world? And what could be more helpful to that mission of our nation than to rid America of its last blot of colonialism by admitting our only two incorporated territories—Alaska and Hawaii—to the equality they seek, the equality provided by the long-established and only possible formula, namely statehood?

America does not, alas, practice what it preaches, as long as it retains Alaska in colonial vassalage.

Is there any doubt that Alaska is a colony? Is there any question that in its maintenance of Alaska as a territory against the expressed will of its inhabitants, and subject to the accompanying political and economic disadvantages, the United States has been and is guilty of colonialism?

Lest there be such doubt, lest there be those who would deny this indictment, let the facts be submitted to a candid world.

You will note that this last sentence is borrowed from that immortal document, the Declaration of Independence. It is wholly appropriate to do this. For, in relation to their time, viewed in the light of mankind's progress in the 180 years since the revolt of the thirteen original American colonies, the "abuses and usurpations" —to use again the language of the Declaration—against which we protest today, are as great, if not greater, than those our revolutionary forbears suffered and against which they revolted.

Let us recall the first item of grievance in the Declaration of Independence:

"He has refused assent to laws, the most wholesome and necessary for the public good."

"He," of course, was King George the Third. Put in his place, in place of the "he", his contemporary equivalent, our ruler, the federal government.

Has it, or has it not, "refused assent to laws most wholesome and necessary for the public good?"

We Alaskans know that the answer is emphatically, "Yes, it has."

He, or for the purpose of 1955, *it,* the federal government, has "refused assent," although requested to do so for some forty years, to the following "most wholesome and necessary laws:"

First. A law transferring the control and management of Alaska's greatest natural resource, the fisheries, to the Territory of

Alaska, as it transferred the corresponding resources to all other Territories in the past.

Second. It has "refused assent" to a law repealing the thirty-five year old discrimination in the Maritime Law of 1920, the "Jones Act," a discrimination uniquely against Alaska.

Third. It has "refused assent" to a reform of our obsolete and unworkable land laws, which would assist and speed population growth, settlement and development of Alaska. It alone is responsible for over 99% of Alaska being still public domain.

Fourth. It has "refused assent" to a law including Alaska in federal aid highway legislation.

Fifth. It has "refused assent" to a law abolishing the barbarous commitment procedure of Alaska's insane which treats them like criminals and confines them in a distant institution in the states.

Sixth. It has "refused assent" to placing our federal lower court judges, the United States commissioners, on salary, and paying them a living wage.

One could cite other examples of such refusal to assent to "laws most wholesome and necessary for the public good."

But let us instead pass on to the second item for complaint, which is similar to the first, in the Declaration of Independence:

"He has forbidden his Governors to pass laws of immediate and growing importance . . ."

Substitute for the "He", then the British royal executive, the present American federal executive, and substitute for "his governors", his party leaders in Congress, and recall their vote in the House of Representatives last May 10, killing a law "of immediate and growing importance"—the statehood bill.

Let us go still further down the list of our revolutionary forefathers' expressed grievances, again quoting the Declaration of Independence:

"He has obstructed the administration of Justice, by refusing his assent to laws establishing judiciary powers."

"He", is today the whole federal government. It has for a decade "obstructed the administration of justice" in Alaska by refusing assent to establishing additional judiciary powers, where they were needed, namely in the Third Judicial Division, while repeatedly increasing the number of judges in the "mother country," the 48 states. And although the population of Alaska has more than tripled in the last forty-six years, the number of federal judges established in Alaska in 1909 remains unchanged. And federal judges are the only judges this colony is permitted to have.

Let us look still further in the Declaration of Independence:

"He has affected to render the military independent and superior to the civil power."

Is there much difference between this and the recent presidential declaration that the defense of Alaska, that is to say the rule of the military here, could be better carried out if Alaska remains a Territory?

One could go on at length drawing the deadly parallels which caused our revolutionary forefathers to raise the standard of freedom, although, clearly, some of the other abuses complained of in that distant day no longer exist.

But Alaska is no less a colony than were those thirteen colonies along the Atlantic seaboard in 1775. The colonialism which the United States imposes on us and which we have suffered for 88 years, is no less burdensome, no less unjust, than that against which they poured out their blood and treasure. And while most Alaskans know that full well, we repeat:

"To prove this let the facts be submitted to a candid world."

To begin at the beginning, the Treaty of Cession by which Alaska was annexed, contained a solemn and specific commitment:

"The inhabitants of the ceded territory . . . shall be admitted to the enjoyment of all the rights, advantages and immunities of citizens of the United States . . ."

That was the pledge. The United States has not kept that pledge. Yet a treaty is the highest law of the land. And it is made in the clear view of all mankind.

The United States has broken that pledge for 88 years. It has not admitted the inhabitants of Alaska to the enjoyment of "all the rights, advantages and immunities of citizens of the United States."

"All the rights, advantages and immunities of citizens of the United States" would entitle us to vote for President and Vice-President, to representation in the Congress by two Senators and a Representative with a vote, and would free us from the restrictions imposed by the Organic Act of 1912, and the Act of Congress of July 30, 1886. Obviously we have neither the vote, nor the representation, nor the freedom from restrictions.

We suffer taxation without representation, which is no less "tyranny" in 1955 than it was in 1775. Actually it is much worse in 1955 than in 1775 because the idea that it was "tyranny" was then new. Since the Revolutionaries abolished it for the states a century and three-quarters ago, it has become a national synonym for something repulsive and intolerable.

We are subject to military service for the nation—a privilege and obligation we accept gladly—yet we have not voice in the making and ending of the wars into which our young men are drafted.

In this respect we are worse off than our colonial forefathers. King George III did not impose conscription upon them. They were not drafted to fight for the mother country. Therefore there was no revolutionary slogan "no conscription without representation." But it is a valid slogan for Alaskans today.

The treaty obligation of 1867 is an obligation to grant us the full equality of statehood, for which Alaskans did not press in the first 80 years of their subordination, but which now, overdue, they demand as their right.

But that is only a small part of the evidence of our colonialism under the American flag. Let us submit more facts to a candid world.

First, let us ask, what is a colony? And let us answer that question.

A colony has been defined in a standard college text-book by a

Columbia University professor as "a geographic area held for political, strategic and economic advantage."

That, as the facts will show, is precisely what the Territory of Alaska is—"a geographic area held for political, strategic and economic advantage."

The maintenance and exploitation of those political, strategic and economic advantages by the holding power is colonialism.

The United States is that holding power.

Inherent in colonialism is an inferior political status.

Inherent in colonialism is an inferior economic status.

The inferior economic status is a consequence of the inferior political status.

The inferior economic status results from discriminatory laws and practices imposed upon the colonials through the superior political strength of the colonial power in the interest of its own non-colonial citizens.

The economic disadvantages of Alaskans which in consequence of such laws and practices redound to the advantage of others living in the states who prosper at the expense of Alaskans—these are the hall-marks of colonialism.

Let us take a look at these hall-marks of colonialism deeply engraved on the policies of the United States in Alaska in the field of transportation. Transportation is the key to almost all development. None have demonstrated this better than have the Americans within the non-colonial areas of their 48 states where transportation of every kind—railways, highways, airways—have linked, built and developed a dynamic domain of continental dimensions.

First, let us scrutinize sea-borne transportation. It was, for seventy-three years, until 1940, the only form of transportation between Alaska and the states. Alaska suffers a unique discrimination in maritime law.

Thirty-five years ago the Congress passed a merchant marine act which is known officially as the Maritime Act of 1920. In Alaska it is referred to as the "Jones Act," after its sponsor, the late Senator Wesley L. Jones of the state of Washington. The act embodied a substantial modification of existing maritime law. It provided that goods shipped across the United States, destined either for the coastal ports of the Atlantic or Pacific or for shipment across those oceans to Europe or to Asia, could use either American or foreign carriers. The foreign carriers principally involved were Canadian.

For example, a shipper from the Atlantic seaboard or from the industrial cities of the middle west of products destined for points to the west could ship these across the country wholly on American railroads or on Canadian railroads, or partly on either.

And when these goods arrived at their Coast destination, he could send them across the Pacific in either American or foreign vessels, or southward in either. But at that point in the legislation, creating this new beneficial arrangement, two words had been inserted in Article 27 of the Act. Those two words were, "excluding Alaska."

Now what did those two words signify? They signified that Alaska, alone among the nations, or possessions of nations, on earth, was denied the advantages afforded all other areas. The same discrimination, obviously, applies to products shipped *from* Alaska.

What was the purpose of this discrimination? Its purpose was to subject Alaska to steamship service owned in the city of Seattle. Senator Jones no doubt assumed, and correctly that this would be most helpful to some of his constituents there, as indeed it proved to be, but at the expense, the heavy expense, from that time on, of our voteless citizens of Alaska.

This was in 1920. Under the limited self-government which Congress had granted Alaska through the Organic Act of 1912, more limited than had been granted any other territory, Alaska was still a youngster. Nevertheless, the fifth Territorial legislature meeting the next year, 1921, protested strenuously against this specific and flagrant discrimination, and ordered the Territorial Attorney-General to take the matter to court. The Territorial legislators believed, and so expressed themselves, that this new legislation enacted by Congress at the behest of Senator Jones of Seattle, was in violation of the commerce clause of the Constitution, which forbids discrimination against any port of the United States.

The case came to the Supreme Court of the United States on an appeal from a decree of the United States District Court dismissing the suit brought by the Territory and by an Alaskan shipper, the Juneau Hardware Company, which sought to restrain the Collector of Customs in Alaska from confiscating merchandise ordered by the hardware company and others in Alaska from points in the United States shipped over Canadian railroads, through Canadian ports and thence to Alaska by Canadian vessels, or merchandise to be shipped from Alaska to the United States in like manner.

In pleading the cause of the Territory, Alaska's Attorney-General John Rustgard argued that both the Treaty provisions and the specific extension of the Constitution to Alaska by the Organic Act of 1912 rendered the discriminatory clause unconstitutional. It looked like a clear case.

The Government—our government—which was defending this discriminatory maritime Act, was represented by the Solicitor-General of the United States, the Honorable James M. Beck of Pennsylvania.

Let the candid world note well the language of his argument:

"The immunity from discrimination is a reserved right on the part of the constituent states . . . The clear distinction of governmental power between states and territories must be constantly borne in mind . . . If the fathers had anticipated the control of the United States over the far-distant Philippine Islands, would they, who concern the reserved rights of the states, have considered for a moment a project that any special privilege which the interests of the United States might require for the ports of entry of the several states should by compulsion be extended to the ports of entry of the colonial dependencies . . .?"

Let the candid world note that the case for the United States was presented on the basis that discrimination against a colonial dependency was proper and legitimate and that "any special privilege" required in the United States would supersede any obligation to a colonial dependency. The colonial dependency involved was and is Alaska.

Mr. Justice McReynolds, in rendering the decision of the court, declared:

"The Act does give preference to the ports of the States over those of the Territories," but, he added, the Court could "find nothing in the Constitution itself or its history which compels the conclusion that it was intended to deprive Congress of the power so to Act."

So it was definitely established by the highest court of the land that Congress had discriminated against Alaska, but that, since Alaska was a colonial dependency, such discrimination was permissible and legal.

Every plea by our Alaska legislatures over a period of 35 years to rectify this grave and unjust discrimination has been ignored by successive Congresses. They have "refused assent" to every attempt by Alaska's delegates to secure remedial legislation.

Now the question naturally arises whether this discrimination imposed by the legislative branch of the federal government, approved by the executive branch, and sanctified by the judicial branch, was to prove to be more than a mere statement of the legality of such discrimination. Was it more than a mere affirmation of the subordinate and inferior status of Alaska's colonials as compared with the dominating and superior status of the American citizens of the states? Did this discrimination also carry with it economic disadvantages? Indeed it did.

Several private enterprises in Alaska were immediately put out of business by the action of Congress in 1920 even before the Supreme Court upheld the legality of that Congressional action.

A resident of Juneau had established a mill to process Sitka spruce. He was paying the required fees to the Forest Service and had developed a market for his product in the Middle West where it was used in airplane manufacture. He was shipping it through Vancouver, where it cost him five dollars a thousand to ship by rail to his customers.

The "Jones Act" automatically compelled him to ship his spruce boards by way of Seattle. Here he was charged eleven dollars a thousand, as against the five dollars he had been paying, plus some additional charges, which totalled more than his profit. In consequence his mill was shut down and a promising infant industry, utilizing an abundant but little used Alaskan resource was extinguished. Not only did the "Jones Act" destroy this and other enterprises, but prevented still others from starting and has prevented them ever since. If anyone doubts that political control of the Territory through remote forces and absentee interests does not cause economic damage to the people of Alaska he need but look at the working of the maritime legislation directed against Alaska and Alaska only.

Its immediate effects were to more than triple the cost of handling Alaska freight in Seattle on purchases made in Seattle, as compared with Seattle-brought cargoes destined for the Orient. Alaska's delegate, at that time, the late Dan Sutherland, testified that the Seattle terminal charges on shipments to Hawaii or Asia were only thirty cents a ton, and all handling charges were absorbed by the steamship lines, the result of competition between Canadian and American railways and steamship lines. But for Alaska, where Congressional legislation had eliminated competition, the Seattle terminal charges on local shipments, that is to say, on goods bought in Seattle destined for Alaska, were one hundred percent higher, or sixty cents a ton wharfage. So Alaskans paid $1.10 a ton for what cost Hawaiians and Asiatics thirty cents a ton—nearly four times as much.

This was by no means all. On shipments anywhere in the United States through Seattle, and destined for points in the Pacific *other* than Alaska, the total handling charges were only thirty cents a ton wharfage, and all other costs were absorbed by railroad and steamship lines. But for identical shipments consigned to Alaska, an unloading charge of sixty-five cents a ton was imposed, plus a wharfage charge of fifty cents a ton, plus a handling charge from wharf to ship of sixty cents a ton. These charges aggregated over five times the cost to a shipper to other points in the Pacific, and had to be paid by the Alaska consignee or shipper, and of course ultimately by the Alaskan consumer.

These damaging figures were presented by Delegate Sutherland at a public congressional committee hearing and made part of the official printed record. No attempt was made by the representatives of the benefitting state-side interests, either then or later, to explain, to justify, to palliate, to challenge, to refute, or to deny his facts.

If there is a clearer and cruder example of colonialism anywhere let it be produced! Here is a clear case where the government of the United States—through its legislative branch which enacted the legislation, the executive branch, through the President, who signed it, and the judicial branch, which through its courts, upheld it—imposed a heavy financial burden on Alaskans exclusively, for the advantage of private business interests in the "mother country."

Nor is even this by any means all on the subject of railroad and steamship discrimination against Alaska, and Alaska alone. In addition to all the above extortions against Alaska's shippers, suppliers and consumers—the direct result of discriminatory legislation —all the railroads of the United States charge a higher rate, sometimes as much as one hundred per cent higher for shipping goods across the continent, if these goods are destined for Alaska.

There is a so-called rail export tariff and a rail import tariff, which apply to a defined geographic area with exceptions made for other areas, which penalizes Alaska and Alaska alone.

Please note that the service rendered by those railroads, for the same distance, is exactly the same, whether the article to be shipped goes ultimately to Alaska or elsewhere in the Pacific or whether it stays on the mainland of the United States. But the charges for Alaska, and Alaska only, on that identical article, for identical mileage, and identical service, are specifically higher, sometimes up to one hundred per cent higher.

This abuse, as well as the others dating from the Jones Act have been the subject of unceasing protest from Alaskans. Alaska's legislatures have repeatedly memorialized the Congress and the federal executive agencies asking for equal treatment. Again and again have Alaska's delegates sought to have the discriminatory clause in the maritime law repealed. But each time the lobbies of the benefitting stateside interests have been successful in preventing any relief action.

How powerful these lobbies are and how successful they have been in maintaining these burdensome manifestations of colonialism may be judged from the unsuccessful efforts of the late Senator Hugh Butler of Nebraska to get the discriminatory words "excluding Alaska" stricken from the Act. He introduced a bill for that purpose.

In a speech on the Senate floor on December 4, 1947, he denounced "the discrimination against the territory in the present law", that is the Maritime Act of 1920, and urged that there was "need for the prompt removal of that discrimination if we are to demonstrate that we are in earnest in our determination to promote the development of Alaska."

In a subsequent communication to Senator Homer Capehart, who was then chairman of a sub-committee on Alaska matters of the Committee on Interstate and Foreign Commerce to which Senator Butler's bill was referred, Senator Butler specified the character and extent of the abuse which Alaska was suffering, saying:

"To-day after 27 years of operation under the Jones Act of 1920, the carriers have failed to establish satisfactory service. . . . The Territory is still without adequate transportation to meet its needs. . . . Most Alaskan coastal towns are not connected with the continental United States, or with each other, by highway or rail. Accordingly they have been at the mercy of a steamship monopoly of long duration. There could be no competition from rail or bus lines which would compel better services or lower rates. American steamship lines have not been able or willing to meet Alaska's transportation requirements. The service has been infrequent and the rates exorbitant."

This caustic language was Senator Butler's. And his testimony and vigorous denunciation are highly significant, not merely because he was very conservative, but because for the first fourteen years of his Senatorial service he was a bitter opponent of statehood for Alaska, a stand which made him the beau ideal of the anti-statehood elements within and without the Territory. He professed conversion to statehood for Alaska in 1954 only a few months before his death. He was still an unqualified opponent of Alaskan statehood when he issued this devastating indictment of the maritime transportation in 1947 and 8.

After going into further detail on the injurious effects on Alaska of the Jones Act, and the fact that most of the "merchandise . . .

food products . . . and other commodities" shipped to Alaska were "an exclusive Seattle prerogative," Senator Butler continued:

"The passage of this amendment to the Jones Act could well mean the difference between the slow, continued strangulation of Alaska's economy, and the full development of the Territory's vast potentialities."

Senator Butler then spoke of the discriminatory rates in favor of canned salmon, which industry, he pointed out, likewise centered in and around Seattle, saying:

"The people of Alaska have long been subject to higher rates than has the salmon industry, for general cargo. These higher rates are, in fact, a decree penalizing the resident Alaskan for living in Alaska; the lower rates are, in effect, a decree requiring the Alaska resident to make up for whatever deficits accrue from the costs of shipping canned salmon and salmon-cannery needs. . . . The strangling provisions of the present laws would be eliminated by the enactment of S. 1834."

S. 1834 was Senator Butler's bill to remove this manifestation of colonialism.

And Senator Butler concluded:

"The development of Alaska would be accelerated, and justice would be done to those permanent residents of our northwestern frontier, who have, for so many years, struggled valiantly against discouraging circumstances to develop that area."

Despite Senator Butler's powerful position as the Chairman of the Committee on Interior and Insular Affairs when his party controlled the Congress, this legislation failed. It did not even come out of committee. Eight more years have passed since that time; the tragic situation as far as Alaska is concerned, in its key transportation, has further deteriorated. Steamship freight rates have continued to go up and up, far above the levels that Senator Butler termed "exorbitant."

Invariably, whenever the operators announced another rate increase, the Alaska territorial authorities used to request the maritime regulatory agency to secure an audit of the company's books in order to demonstrate that the increases requested where justified. But almost invariably the increases were granted without such audit and often without question. It may well be asked whether, if Alaska were not a colony, but a State, its two Senators might not be reasonably effective in at least securing a demonstration from the carrier that its financial situation justified the rate increase demanded and promptly acceded to by the federal maritime bureau.

But actually, if Alaska were a State, the whole discrimination in the Jones Act would go out of the port-hole. Alaska would then get the same treatment in the transportation of freight that is accorded to every other area under the flag and to foreign countries. But as a colony it gets no consideration in this matter either from the legislative branch, the Congress, or from the executive branch, in this instance the Federal Maritime Board, successor to other agencies similarly subservient to the vested interests within the colonial power.

The net result of those cumulative charges—50 to 100 per cent higher railroad freight rates to Seattle, higher unloading and transfer charges in Seattle, higher wharfage and higher longshoring charges, and finally higher maritime freight rates to Alaska ports —all higher than anywhere else for any but Alaskans, has been and is greatly to increase the cost of living in Alaska. This in itself has been and continues to be a great hindrance to settlement and permanent residence in Alaska, a heavy burden on private enterprise in Alaska, a forecloser of new enterprise, and obviously a great obstacle to development.

How absurd in the light of these facts—and others similar to be submitted to our candid world—is the allegation of the small minority of Alaskans and of others "outside" that we are not ready for statehood. How shall we get readier with these handicaps? How can we cope with what conservative Senator Butler described as "the slow, continued strangulation of Alaska's economy," if the throttling grip of colonialism is not loosened?

To complete the maritime picture, beginning last year all passenger travel on American boats has ceased. The Alaska Steamship Line has eliminated it. This is a blow to an infant and potentially great industry in Alaska, the tourist industry, which four years ago the Alaska 1951 legislature sought to develop by establishing the Alaska Visitors' Association, financed jointly by territorially appropriated and publicly subscribed funds.

One postscript remains on the subject of maritime transportation before we pass on to other of Alaska's colonial disadvantages. Though it is invariably pointed out by Congressional opponents of statehood that Alaska is a non-contiguous area, separated from the main body of the 48 states by some 700 miles of foreign territory, or 700 miles of either international or foreign coastal waters, the United States persists in maintaining the coast-wise shipping laws against Alaska. Their removal would make a steamship line eligible for the subsidies which American flag ships in the European, African or Asiatic trade receive. That might, were Congress sufficiently interested, induce some competition in the Alaska steamship trade from other American carriers. That the imposition of the coast-wise shipping laws is not ˙a necessary corollary to being a colony, it proved by the fact that the United States has suspended the coastwise shipping laws for the Virgin Islands. But it has declined to do so for Alaska.

Let us now turn to a third form of transportation: highways. These catchwords of colonialism, "excluding Alaska", likewise apply to our highway transportation. For Alaska is denied inclusion in the Federal Aid Highway Act. From this beneficent legislation enacted in 1916, and repeatedly amended and amplified, Alaska, alone among the States and incorporated territories, is excluded. Even Puerto Rico, which pays no federal taxes whatever, is included. Yet Alaskans pay all taxes, including the federal gas tax.

The Congressionally wrought substitute—annual appropriation—is a witness to colonialism expressed in cold figures. The results are visible in the lack of an adequate Alaskan highway system. After 88 years of colonialism and 40 years after the enactment by Congress of the joint federal aid and state highway program, Alaska has only some 3,500 miles of highway. This is a negligible amount for an area one-fifth as large as the 48 states and with only one railroad.

For the first 38 years after the cession of Alaska no roads were built by any government agency. With Alaska almost totally public domain, highway construction was clearly a federal responsibility. In the next 36 years beginning with the first federal construction in 1905 and the outbreak of World War II, in 1941, the federal government appropriated about nineteen and a half million dollars, an average of a trifle over half a million dollars a year—a pittance. During that same period Alaska contributed some nine million dollars. Thus the federal contribution was 68.4 per cent of the total of twenty-eight and a half million dollars, and Alaska's was 31.6 per cent, a far greater proportion than Alaska with its virtual totality of public domain would have had to pay under the Federal Aid Highway Act. It is fair to say, however, that under the Highway Act, federal funds go for construction and not for maintenance.

After road construction had been transferred from the War Department to the Department of the Interior in 1930, for the next decade or more throughout the nineteen thirties, when the federal government and the States were jointly expanding the national highway network, Alaska was given no new highway construction. Maintenance only was granted. Military requirements brought the Alaska Highway and the Glenn Highway, and in the later 1940's a highway program to satisfy defense needs was begun and carried out for five years. But even that has been brought to a virtual halt. For the past three years the federal program has contained no new highway project. This year a token appropriation was included for the desirable Fairbanks-Nenana road, but at the price of halting construction of the important Copper River Highway. In fact the present greatly reduced program spells little more than slow completion and paving of the military highways begun eight years ago. The federal government seems to be heading us back to mere maintenance.

In contrast the federal aid program in the mother country is being handsomely increased, reaching the largest sums in its history in the current biennial appropriation enacted in the second session of the 83rd Congress.

If Alaska were a State it would be automatically included in the expanding highway program. But as a colony it continues to be discriminated against, and that discrimination, instead of lessening is being aggravated.

By the same token Alaska has been excluded from the administration's one hundred and one billion dollar federal highway program. One of its principal justifications, perhaps the principal justification, for this lavish, yet important and valuable proposal, is that it is in part a civilian defense measure to aid evacuation and dispersal in the event of a shooting war with atomic weapons. Yet the same administration that excludes Alaska from this defense measure wishes to keep Alaska in colonial bondage because of alleged national defense reasons.

The enactment of this multi-billion dollar program was deferred in the last session of Congress because of differences of opinion on how to finance it. But in one respect there was no difference of opinion: Alaska would be taxed for the program even if not included in it. The Eisenhower program, presented by General Lucius Clay, called for long term bonding to be repaid out of general funds, Congressional substitutes, on a more nearly "pay-as-you-go" basis, called for increased taxes on gasoline, tires, and other automobile accessories. Efforts to include Alaska in both programs failed, as did subsequent efforts to exclude Alaska from the tax provisions. So Alaskans will be taxed for benefits accruing solely to the residents of the mother country. What else is this but colonialism, crude, stark, undisguised and unashamed?

When both the presidential and congressional drafts failed of passage, President Eisenhower declared he was "deeply disappointed" and added:

"The nation badly needs good roads. The good of our people, of our economy, and of our defense requires that the construction of these highways be undertaken at once."

As colonials we can merely note that Alaskans are, in the consideration of our President, apparently not part of "our people, our economy and our defense."

There is yet more of humiliating disregard. The federal administration while patently uninterested in developing Alaska through its highways is strongly in favor of completing the Inter-American Highway.

On March 31, last, President Eisenhower in a letter to Vice-President Nixon requested an increase in the current appropriation for the central American portion from five million to seventy-five million dollars, a more than thirteen-fold increase. The President gave several reasons for this massive amplification. Three of them emphasized the important economic contribution to the countries through which this highway passes, and a fourth stressed the security aspects of the road.

We may applaud the purpose to complete the Inter-American Highway, with its economic benefits to Guatemala, Honduras, Salvador, Costa Rica, Nicaragua and Panama. We may even enjoy our participation in this philanthropy to these good neighbors, remembering that it is more blessed to give than to receive, and that every Alaskan is paying his share of that 75 million dollars. Still, some of us may wonder why similar consideration is not vouchsafed to Alaska, whose highway and economic needs are great, whose trade is almost exclusively with the United States, and whose relation to national security is certainly much closer than that of the Central American republics. This wonder in our part would be particularly natural since President Eisenhower seems to exhibit concern about Alaska's defense in connection with statehood.

We have now viewed three flagrant examples of colonialism in three of the major means of transportation, shipping, railways and highways. Let us now look at the fourth—airways.

It is superfluous to signalize our air-mindedness to any group of Alaskans. But the candid world should know that Alaskans fly thirty to forty times more than other Americans, and starting with our bush pilots, early developed a fine system of intra-Alaskan aviation. It was almost wholly an Alaskan enterprise— flown and financed by Alaskans—though for a time without airports, aids to navigation and other assistance provided in the mother country. The Air Commerce Act of 1926—a sort of federal aid act for air—did not supply any of these aids to Alaska, although Alaska was included in the legislation. Nevertheless Alaska again suffered the penalty of being a colony, this time at the hands of the federal executive agency entrusted with administration of the Act. This time it was the bureaucrats who "excluded" Alaska. But the Alaskan bush pilots flew anyhow and what we have in the way of airways in Alaska is largely due to their courageous and skilful pioneering.

However, air service between Alaska and the States, which required the approval of federal bureaus and investment of outside capital, lagged far behind. The first commercial service connecting Alaska with the mother country did not take place til 1940, long after American commercial air carriers had spanned the rest of the hemisphere and had established regular service across the Pacific.

Meanwhile the newly created bureaucracies óf the Civil Aeronautics Board and the Civil Aeronautics Administration moved into Alaska. They began restricting local enterprise. In the late 1940's, over the widespread protests of Alaskans, the C. A. B. began cracking down on non-scheduled operations, and finally eliminated the "non-scheds" completely. It did not do so in the forty-eight states. Alaska was again the victim of its colonial status. We had no Senators or voting representatives to fend for us.

The successive certification cases which for over a decade have dealt with transportation between the states and Alaska, have been desperate, and not wholly successful, struggles by Alaskans to overcome the inadequate understanding of the Civil Aeronautics Board that air transportation is relatively much more important in Alaska than in the states with their well-established alternative forms of transportation, by railways and highways. Five years ago interior Alaska was saved from insufficient service only by President Truman's overruling the Board and granting certification to one of the two Alaskan carriers which the Board had denied.

For the last two years our two Alaskan carriers, in the face of steadily mounting traffic, have managed by heroic, all-out effort at least to retain what they had. But it is noteworthy that while the two international carriers serving Alaska, both "mother country" enterprises, have been granted permanent certificates, the certificates for our two Alaskan carriers are only temporary—a handicap to their financing and to their ability to expand.

Alaska's statehood case could rest here. Yet no account of its 88 years would be complete without some notice of the salmon fishery. It comes, this year, pretty close to being an obituary notice.

Here was Alaska's greatest natural resource.

Here was the nation's greatest fishery resource.

For nearly half a century, the federal government has totally ignored, has "refused assent" to the petitions, pleas, prayers, memorials, of legislatures, delegates, governors, and of the whole Alaskan people for measures that would conserve that resource.

The result is written in figures that spell tragedy for Alaska's fishermen and for many others in Alaska's coastal communities whose economy has long depended on the fisheries. The tragedy has deepened year after year. So grave has become the plight that the administration found it necessary to proclaim the fishing villages to be disaster areas. It is a disaster caused by colonialism, and the federal government may charge the costs of disaster relief and loss of federal tax income to its own policies.

From over eight million cases twenty years ago the salmon pack has fallen year by year until in 1955 it has reached the incredible low of 2,382,131 cases, the lowest in 46 years.

Nowhere, as in the Alaska fisheries fiasco, is the lesson clearer or the superiority, in purely material terms, of self-government to colonialism. In neighboring British Columbia and Washington State, where the fisheries are under home rule, and where fish traps have been abolished, the identical resource has not only been conserved but augmented.

It is colonialism that has both disregarded the interest of the Alaskan people and caused the failure of the prescribed federal conservation function. Colonialism has preferred to conserve the power and perquisites of a distant bureaucracy and the control and special privileges—the fish traps—of a politically potent absentee industry. Alaska has been the victim, but the entire nation has also lost heavily.

Let us by way of a footnote make crystal clear how and why this is colonialism—because some defenders of the *status quo* may deny it is, and we don't want the candid world to be confused.

The people of Alaska have repeatedly and unchangingly manifested their overwhelming opposition to fish traps. It isn't necessary to rehearse all their reasons—the results have amply justified the Alaskans' position. But fish trap beneficiaries, residents of the mother country, want to retain their Alaska traps. So the traps are retained. And it is the power and authority of the federal government which retains them. In a clear-cut issue between the few, profiting, non-colonial Americans and the many, seriously damaged, colonial Alaskans, the state-side interest wins hands down. And it wins because the government, which is also supposed to be *our* government, throws its full weight on their side and against us. *That* is colonialism.

It would be impossible in any one address, even one that assumed the length of a Senate filibuster, to list all the wrongs, disadvantages and lack of immunities that Alaska has endured in its 88 years as a territory. They constitute an incredible story. Even for these who know it, it is hard to believe. It is hard for us as Americans who long ago established our faith in American intelligence, competence, good sense, and above all in American fair play, to contemplate the story of American colonialism in Alaska. It has been part of our faith, an abiding faith, that to right deep-seated wrongs in America, one but had to make them sufficiently widely known. And our best hope does lie, I am convinced, in making the facts known widely—and especially the overshadowing fact of our colonialism—to our fellow-Americans and to the rest of the candid world. They should know that what progress has been made in Alaska, and it has been substantial and praiseworthy, has been made in spite of these colonial impositions, and largely because of the character and fibre of the colonials themselves. Coming here from the forty-eight states, following the most cherished American trend, the westward march in search of greater freedom and greater opportunity, they brought to the last frontier and to its friendly native population, the very qualities that have made America. Only distantly man-made problems, the problems created by a remote, often unseen officialdom and its beneficiaries in the mother country, have remained unresolved.

Alaskans have striven consistently to resolve them. Let it be recorded that for 43 years, since the first legislature, and before that by individuals and groups, they have pleaded for relief from the abuses a part of which have been detailed.

Yet after two generations not a single one of these pleas, all of them fair and reasonable, has been granted.

How applicable to Alaska's plight the words of the Declaration of Independence:

"In every stage of these oppressions we have petitioned for redress in the most humble terms. Our repeated petitions have been answered by repeated injury."

Lest these frequent citations from the Declaration of Independence lead anyone to the conclusion that there are any among us who now desire our independence, let such a totally erroneous assumption be promptly corrected. We desire and demand an end to our colonialism. But we seek it through a re-affirmation in deeds for Alaska of the principles which launched the American experiment, and re-application of the practice that has been followed in 35 states.

We Alaskans believe—passionately—that American citizenship is the most precious possession in the world. Hence we want it in full measure; full citizenship instead of half-citizenship; first class instead of second class citizenship. We demand equality with all other Americans, and the liberties, long denied us, that go with it. To adapt Daniel Webster's famous phrase uttered as a peroration against impending separatism, we Alaskans want "liberty *and* union, one and inseparable, now and forever."

But the keepers of Alaska's colonial status should be reminded that the 18th century colonials for long years sought merely to obtain relief from abuses, for which they—like us—vainly pleaded, before finally resolving that only independence would secure for them the "life, liberty and pursuit of happiness," which they felt was their natural right.

We trust that the United States will not by similar blindness to our rights and deafness to our pleas drive Alaskans from patient hope to desperation.

We have been challenged in the course of Congressional debates to show as a pre-requisite that admission of Alaska to statehood would be beneficial to the nation. That test was never applied to earlier territories seeking and securing statehood. But we gladly accept that challenge and willingly subscribe to it as a condition.

The development of Alaska, the fulfillment of its great destiny, cannot be achieved under colonialism. The whole nation will profit by an Alaska that is populous, prosperous, strong, self-reliant—a great northern and western citadel of the American idea. Statehood would automatically bring us far along that high road.

Nothing could more pathetically reveal the lack of understanding regarding Alaska, and the poor advice concerning Alaska that is given and accepted in the highest places, than the presidential pronouncement in the last state-of-the-union message.

"As the complex problems of Alaska are resolved that Territory should expect to achieve statehood."

Bless us! The complex problems of Alaska are inherent in its territorial status; they are derived from its colonial status; they will be largely resolved by statehood and only by statehood.

As was promptly called to President Eisenhower's attention this was like the old story of telling a youngster he must learn to swim before going into the water!

So we return to the proposition that America can scarcely afford to perpetuate its colonialism. Our nation is attempting to lead the world into the pathway of peace. No goal could be more worthy. But to lead effectively, it must not only practice what it preaches. It must carry out its solemn commitments. It can scarcely be critical of nations that break their pledges and break its own. It must first cast the beam out of its own eye before attempting to pull the motes of its neighbors' eyes.

For the United States has pledged its good name and good faith in treaties and agreements far more recent than the Treaty of Cession of 1867. Not that our nation's responsibility for not carrying out those original pledges in regard to Alaska is diminished by the passage of time. But there are recent and even contemporary commitments which demand fulfillment.

Article 73 of the United Nations Charter, dealing with non-selfgoverning territories—and that includes Alaska which must make annual reports to the U.N.—pledges the signatories:

"To the principle that the interests of the inhabitants of these territories is paramount," and further pledges them

"To insure . . . their political, economic, social, and educational advancement, their just treatment, and their protection against abuses," and, finally, and this is most pertinent, it pledges them

"To develop self-government, to take due account of the political aspirations of the peoples and to assist them in the progressive development of their free political institutions. . . ."

The United States pledged itself to that ten years ago. If the English language has not lost its meaning and the United States its integrity, it should some time ago have, and should now, in any event, "take due account of the political aspirations" of Alaskans and enable them to develop the self-government which they seek.

There is an even more recent commitment—the Pacific charter—signed a year ago, in which the signatory nations, including the United States, pledged themselves "to uphold the principle of equal rights and self-determination of peoples," and to re-enforce that principle the signatories further pledged that they were "prepared to continue taking effective practical measures to insure conditions favorable to orderly achievement of the foregoing purposes", namely self-government.

We are agreed that there is only one form of self-government that is possible for Alaska. And so we are drawing up the constitution for the State that we fervently hope will soon come to be. That hope, it is encouraging to note, is shared by the great majority of Americans. If our 88-year experience inevitably leads to strictures of the colonialism that has ruled us, let us remember that it is a course not sanctioned by American public opinion. The Gallup polls, which last recorded an 82 per cent support of Alaskan statehood, the endorsement of virtually every important national organization, demonstrate clearly that the forces in and out of government which would deny Alaska statehood—in fact the government itself—do not represent prevailing American sentiment.

But while we may derive satisfaction and hope there-from, let us not delude ourselves that victory is at hand. It ought to be. But too many solemn pledges to Alaska have been honored in the breach to assure that what ought to be will be.

It may be regrettable—or not—but every generation must fight to preserve its freedom. We have twice in a life-time participated in our nation's fight to preserve them. In Alaska we still have to win them.

This Constitutional Convention is an important mobilization. But the battle still lies ahead, and it will require all our fortitude, audacity, resoluteness—and maybe something more—to achieve victory. When the need for that something more comes, if we have the courage—the guts—to do whatever is necessary, we shall not fail. That the victory will be the nation's as well as Alaska's—and the world's—should deepen our determination to end American colonialism.

President Eisenhower signs — on January 3, 1959 — the proclamation admitting Alaska as the 49th State. Witnessing the signing are from left to right: Representative Ralph J. Rivers, Senator Ernest Gruening, Senator E. L. (Bob) Bartlett, Secretary of the Interior Fred A. Seaton, Acting Governor of Alaska Waino Hendrickson, David W. Kendall, special counsel to the President, Mike Stepovich, former Governor of Alaska, Robert B. Atwood, Editor and Publisher of *Anchorage Times.*

Cheering group in the Capitol just after passage of Statehood bill in Senate, June 30, 1958. Left to right, Senator Warren Magnuson, Ernest Gruening, Representative Leo O'Brien, Senator Frank Church, William A. Egan, Senator Thomas Kuchel, Governor Mike Stepovich, Robert Groseclose, Senator Henry M. Jackson, Ralph J. Rivers, Wally Hickel, Senator Arthur Watkins.

VII

T HE Eisenhower opposition to Alaskan statehood, colliding
with its Congressional supporters' determination to get equal
treatment for both Pacific territories, had created an impasse
during the 83rd and 84th Congresses. The opposition was evidenced
in the adverse testimony of administration officials.

Secretary of the Interior Douglas McKay, appearing as the first
witness before the Senate Committee on Interior and Insular Affairs on February 21, 1955, while giving all-out support to Hawaii's
immediate admission, said he did not recommend such action for
Alaska. Similarly adverse was the testimony of Secretary of Defense Charles E. Wilson and Under Secretary of the Air Force
James H. Douglas. Senator Jackson, conducting the hearing, pointed out that "the Defense Department's present position is a direct reversal of that taken by the same Department in 1950 and
1952, and emphasized by the then Commanding General of the
Armed Forces in Alaska, General Nathan F. Twining, in a personal appearance before the committee in 1950."[1]

President Eisenhower's views on statehood, variously expressed
in his messages to the Congress, were more fully revealed in an
interview with Frank Hewlett, Washington correspondent of the
Honolulu *Star*-Bulletin in September, 1956, when the following ex-
change took place:

> "*Frank Hewlett:* Mr. President, the Republican platform calls for
> statehood for Hawaii and Alaska in the strongest terms ever used.
> Would you care to elaborate on the Alaska plank which pledges im-
> mediate statehood for Alaska and then adds the words 'recognizing
> the fact that adequate provisions for defense requirements must be
> made?' "

> "*The President:* Well, I think I have talked about that subject
> ... time and again. As far as Hawaii is concerned, there is no
> question. I not only approved of it in the '52 platform, but time and
> again I brought it before the Congress in the terms of recommenda-
> tions. Now, Alaska, is a very great area, and there are very few peo-
> ple in it, and they are confined almost exclusively to the southeastern
> corner. Could there be a way worked out where the defense require-
> ments could be retained, I mean the areas necessary to defense re-
> quirements could be retained under Federal control in the great out-
> lying regions and a State made of that portion in which the popu-
> lation is concentrated, it would seem to me to be a good solution to
> the problem. But the great and vast area is completely dependent
> upon the United States for protection and it is necessary to us in our
> defense arrangements."

In its leading editorial a few days later, the Fairbanks Daily

News-Miner, a strongly Republican newspaper, commented on this interview as follows:

"President Eisenhower, at a recent news conference, discussed Alaska with reporters. His words, reported in a dispatch from our nation's capital yesterday, reflect shocking ignorance concerning Alaska on the part of the President.

"The President, in discussing Alaska Statehood, told reporters that Alaska has only a small population which is concentrated in the Southeast part of the Territory. He went on to say that there are very few people in the vast remainder of Alaska, and furthermore, this area is vital to U. S. defense. He indicated that possibly some way could be worked out to grant statehood to this populated corner in Southeastern Alaska.

"All of which is most puzzling to us. Alaska's population isn't centered in the Southeastern Area. Alaska's heavily populated region is the railbelt, which extends from Seward in South Central Alaska to Fairbanks, which is close to the Arctic Circle.

"There are some 80,000 people living in the Anchorage, Palmer, Seward, Kenai region, and that is a greater population by far than all of Southeastern Alaska. In addition, there are some 45,000 people living in the Fairbanks-Big Delta and Interior Alaska region. We aren't mentioning Kodiak, Nome or other centers far from Southeastern Alaska.

"There once was a time when Alaska's population was centered in the Southeastern region, but that time was about 25 years ago. Southeastern Alaska is quite healthy economically and growing steadily in population, but it has been outstripped in growth by the railbelt region.

"We wonder who has been advising the President concerning Alaska."

The President's expressed thought of making only part of Alaska a State and reserving the rest of it under Federal control as a defense area, appeared to have its origins in a proposal made two years earlier by Governor B. Frank Heintzleman that the southern and southeastern areas only be admitted to statehood.

His reasoning was that these were the economically viable areas, and that the State should not be burdened with the support and management of the sparsely inhabited northern and western regions. Public opinion in Alaska emphatically rejected this proposal, described as "partition", in the conviction that Alaska was historically and geographically one; that exclusion of any portion of its population would be grossly unfair to it; and that the areas proposed for exclusion were not without economic potentials in sub-soil resources.

Heintzleman told me that the idea had originated solely with him. But before long, it was transmuted by the Eisenhower administration into a proposal that a similar area, roughly the half of Alaska north of the Yukon and Kuskokwim, be reserved for defense purposes and that acceptance of such an amendment to the statehood bill was required to secure the administration's approval of statehood.

An unexpected event would perhaps if not alter, at least slightly deviate, the course of history. Douglas McKay was requested to run for the Senate in Oregon against Wayne Morse, who had switched to the Democratic party. To succeed McKay, President Eisenhower nominated Fred Seaton for the Secretaryship of the Interior.

At the hearing on his confirmation before the Senate Committee on Interior and Insular Affairs, Senator Murray, presiding, promptly placed in the record Seaton's Senate speech on statehood, quoting its pertinent sentences. He then asked whether Seaton still felt hat way about Alaskan statehood.

The answer was afirmative. Subsequently, in response to questions from Senators Richard Neuberger and Henry Jackson, Seaton indicated that "if these withdrawal terms could (can) be worked out" he would do everything he could to convince the President that Alaska should have statehood immediately.

I saw Fred Seaton shortly after my election as an "Alaska-Tennessee Plan" Senator and gave him my view that Alaskans would never go for a partial or partitioned state. I was reassured by my impression that he was as committed as ever to Alaskan statehood and would work for an acceptable compromise. And so it proved. Extensive hearings and close cross-examination of military witnesses made clear that there was virtually nothing in the way of defense withdrawals that the President, as Commander-in-Chief, could not do without excluding any part of Alaska from statehood. What in time amounted to a face-saving formula for the administration was provided as an amendment to the existing statehood bill drafts giving the President the power to make defense withdrawals within the area previously designated. It remained in the Statehood Act (Section 10) and has been meaningless and of no significance ever since.

In the 85th Congress (1957-1959) hearings were resumed in both the Senate and House. The drafts of the statehood bill in both had become steadily more generous than in preceding versions. In the 84th Congress the land to be granted Alaska had been increased to 102,950,000 acres from the vacant unreserved and unappropriated lands of the public domain, plus 400,000 acres from the national forests. Seventy per cent of the net proceeds of the Pribilof seal and sea otter skins would go to the State. Most helpful was the provision that ninety per cent of the royalties and net profits from oil, gas and mineral leases on the public domain would go to Alaska. This unique benefit not enjoyed by the Western States was granted in part in compensation for the fact that Alaska was not—as they were—under the Reclamation Act. Alaska owes this provision to the efforts of the late Senator Frank Barrett, of Wyoming, who insisted that this larger royalty should go to Alaska and that it become part of our Statehood Act.

Senator Barrett's proposal came in the course of my testimony before the Committee on Interior and Insular Affairs on March 25, 1957. It was my feeling that what I had to say, and what others testifying for statehood could say, had been said many times, and it was desirable to terminate the hearings and concentrate on floor action, a view that was shared by Senator Henry M. Jackson, who would be the floor manager of the bill in the Senate, and by Clair Engle, of California, Chairman of the House Committee on Interior and Insular Affairs. However, an unforeseen circumstance led me to testify at length before the House committee.

C. W. Snedden, publisher of the Fairbanks Daily News-Miner, who had purchased the paper from the estate of Austin E. Lathrop after his death and changed its anti-statehood policy to one of militant support, and was personally active in behalf of Statehood, was testifying before the House Committee on March 12th. He had made an excellent statement analyzing some of the handicaps which Alaskans encountered due to their territorial status, saying that "the territorial form of government is un-American, un-democratic, stifling to free enterprise, and damaging to the morale of the people who are being administered." He went into detail on the extra freight charges which were levied exclusively on rail shipments destined for Alaska from any point in the United States to Seattle, on the further high costs of handling goods there, and on the excessive steamship rates to Alaska.

Concluding his remarks, he said: "The second-class American citizens of Alaska ask that you put an end to this neglect now and that you give us a fighting chance to prove our worth and our ability to develop our great Territory as a State in a sound economic climate."

His statement aroused the ire of Representative A. L. Miller, of Nebraska, who, like Senator Butler, his Senate colleague, had always opposed statehood while alleging that his opposition was due to the fact that the particular bill before his committee was not sufficiently generous. He said: "You refer to yourself as being 'second-class citizens . . . I rather resent that statement. I resent the statement that you read into the record as to your 'colonial form of government'. I think it is wrong . . . I don't know why you refer to 'second-class citizens'. It makes me a little hot under the collar." Similar indignation was voiced by Representative James Haley, D., of Florida.

As I felt that the sense of outrage expressed by Representatives Miller and Haley was totally unjustified, both at Snedden's references to our being second-class citizens and the victims of colonialism, which expressed my own view and indeed was the theme of my keynote address to the Constitutional Convention in 1955, I thought I would accept Chairman Engle's invitation to me to testify to make this clear. So, after outlining what seemed to me the solemn treaty commitments and other obligations of the United States dating from the purchase, I said:

> "I did not intend to go into this subject in detail, assuming that the members of the Committee were familiar with it, but since yesterday, when two members of the Committee challenged the testimony of one of our witnesses, Mr. C. W. Snedden, the publisher of the Fairbanks News-Miner, when he said that he considered that we Alaskans were second-class citizens, I wish to say that a great number of Alaskans, perhaps a majority, hold that view with him. I, for one, share it, and I am prepared today to try to document my convic-

tion to that effect. It is my belief that Uncle Sam has been guilty of colonialism in Alaska. Colonialism is an ugly word and is somewhat in disrepute now, but we were born as a nation through revolt against colonialism and I assure you that the grievances of our colonial forefathers were similar in a number of respects to those against which they protested in Alaska, beginning almost 90 years ago, and against which we protest today."

I then proceeded to document my belief further.

Other witnesses at this hearing were: A. W. Boddy, of Juneau, President of the Alaska Sportsmen's Council, who testified to his belief that Alaskans were not capable or mature enough to manage their natural resources; and Glen Franklin, the chairman of the Legislative Committee of the Alaska Miners Association, who stated that he had reservations as to whether the State could pay its way, and that he was not in favor of immediate statehood for Alaska.

However, these last hearings were more or less perfunctory. The fight would be on the floor of both the House and the Senate.

Between sessions of the 85th Congress, in order to try to improve the support from the California delegation, most of whose Democrats favored statehood but most of whose Republicans did not, I felt it desirable to go to the Bay area and see if I couldn't get a resolution of support from the San Francisco and Oakland Chambers of Commerce. In previous years we had enlisted all the other Pacific Coast Chambers except Seattle. So, I arranged to be invited to a luncheon of the Executive Committees of the San Francisco and Oakland Chambers, and succeeded in persuading them of the desirability of endorsing Alaskan statehood.

The refusal of the Seattle Chamber, to the very end, to endorse Alaskan statehood, was merely an evidence that from a certain powerful group in Seattle stemmed the economic colonialism of which Alaska was the victim. It was made crystal-clear to me by an event in 1949 when the people of Seattle suddenly awakened to an impending calamity. The Air Force had decided to move the Boeing plant from Seattle to Wichita, Kansas. Boeing was, at that time, Seattle's largest employer and its oldest big industry, its founding having synchronized almost with the beginnings of aviation.

This removal of Boeing would be a terrible disaster to Seattle. It would mean that the 25,000 employees would either lose their jobs or be obliged to sell their homes and move halfway across the country to entirely new surroundings.

The Seattle Chamber of Commerce organized a big hearing of potential protest, to which it invited the leaders of industry, commerce, labor, and the press, as well as the State of Washington's delegation to the Congress, and for some reason asked me to come down from Juneau. The meeting was held in the ballroom of the Olympic Hotel. Present to explain why this action had been taken was Stuart Symington, the Secretary of the Air Force. He had with him a 3-star General by the name of Kenneth B. Wolfe. In opening the meeting, Secretary Symington explained that this was a military decision that had been made by the 3-star General at his side, but that he approved it, because it was known that the Russians had planes that could fly the 2,400 miles from Eastern Siberia to Puget Sound and return, but that Wichita was 3,600 miles away and hence out of range.

The Washington delegation, which was present with the exception of Senator Harry Cain, who was in the Pacific, pleaded that this was a terrible thing to do but apparently had accepted it as one of those military necessities against which there is no use to argue.

The whole performance struck me as utterly ridiculous because, in the first place, it seemed clear to me that if in a given year planes had a range of twice 2,400 miles, or 4,800, within a very few years that range would be increased and a place much farther away would be no less vulnerable. So, I denounced the project, quoting Georges Clemenceau (although Aristide Briand, I am told, actually said it) that "war is too important a matter to leave to the Generals"; that this was nothing but a twentieth-century retreat from Moscow which would prove as disastrous as Napoleon's had been, and that there were other installations, such as the Atomic Energy Plant at Hanford and Grand Coulee Dam, which could not be moved, and that there had been no report as yet that the Navy proposed to move the Bremerton Navy Yard up the Mississippi. I expressed pain that the Air Force, at that time my favorite branch of the services, since two of my sons had served in it as pilots in World War II, instead of emulating that aggressive bird, the American Eagle, was following the example of lesser birds and pursuing a policy that seemed to be both ostrich-headed and chicken-hearted.

I saw the blood rise in Stu Symington's cheeks at this comment.

Then I went to a map of Alaska hanging there and pointed out that if there were a radar screen around the North and West of Alaska and plenty of interceptor planes, the Russians would never fly the 2,400 miles across Alaska but would be compelled to fly southwest around the Aleutians, and then southeast again, and that then their Boeing target would be 3,600 miles away, not 2,400.

Within a few days the Air Force rescinded its decision, and a few months later, had appropriated $50 million from its funds without going to Congress, to start the D.E.W. Line.

A few days after the announcement that Boeing would not be moved, my wife received a dozen American Beauty roses from the President of the Seattle Chamber of Commerce and I a letter thanking me for what I had done and asking me whether it could do anything for me in return. I replied there was nothing; that this was a mutually satisfactory decision but that since he had mentioned doing something for me, why wouldn't the Seattle Chamber of Commerce adopt a resolution supporting statehood for Alaska? I got a wire the next day from President Nat S. Rogers, saying it would be done immediately. But several days later I received a letter from him saying that he regretted to inform me that on further investigation, he found that all Alaska matters were

always referred to the Alaska Committee and that this committee
had decided that it could not adopt such a resolution because it
would be political.

I wrote in reply: "How come that three years ago the Seattle
Chamber of Commerce approved a resolution endorsing statehood
for Hawaii? That wasn't political! The fact is that the so-called
Alaska Committee is dominated by a handful of men who view
Alaska as King George III and his ministers viewed the thirteen
colonies—as something to be exploited and kept down but never to
be given equality."

I received an invitation from Mr. Rogers to come down to
Seattle and meet with the Executive Committee of the Alaska Committee, but I knew too well who they were and what their views
were and decided it would be a waste of time. And so, to the very
end, even when statehood was inevitable, the Seattle Chamber of
Commerce never endorsed statehood for Alaska while every other
Pacific Coast Chamber had done so.

This picture was taken at the White House on January 3, 1959, after the signing by
the President of the Statehood Proclamation and shows a group celebrating and exhibit-
ing the new 49 star flag, which had just been unveiled. Left to right: Representative
Ralph J. Rivers; Robert B. Atwood, Editor and Publisher of the Anchorage *Times*,
Chairman of the Alaska Statehood Committee; Fred A. Seaton, Secretary of the Interior;
Ernest Gruening; Bob Bartlett; Mike Stepovich, last Territorial Governor of Alaska;
and Waino Hendrickson, Acting Governor in the final months of territorial government.

Texans, in general, were not happy at the admission of a state larger than Texas. In the House vote only four of the Texas delegation voted to support statehood. Both Texas Senators were absent during the Senate vote although Ralph Yarborough was all along an enthusiastic supporter of statehood. Cartoonist Justus of the Minneapolis *Star* portrays the Texans' feeling graphically.

VIII

F OR the next two years, during the first and second sessions of the 85th Congress, our Alaska-Tennessee Plan Delegation— Egan, Gruening, Rivers—called upon every Senator and Representative. The greatest obstacles that we had to overcome were the fact of non-contiguity and the relative smallness of our population. Typical was a conversation I had with a friendly Senator, later converted, who said:

"I am sympathetic with your desire for statehood. I understand why you want it and I think your desires are fully justified. But how can I justify giving this handful of people" (and invariably the reference would be to the 1950 Census, which gave us only 127,000 people, although we knew we had increased to nearly 200,000 by this time) "two Senators when the great State of New York, with 15,-000,000 people, has only two."

Well, we answered by pointing out that if this argument had prevailed in the early days of the Republic, we would still have

Alaska-Tennessee Plan delegation with Governor Frank Clement of Tennessee, left to right: Frank Clement, Ernest Gruening, William Egan, Ralph Rivers.

only the 13 original States, since the subsequent States West of the Appalachians invariably had far fewer people than those already in; and second, that we in Alaska would not get more population until we had statehood.

One Senator, who was unalterably opposed, would analyze our population based again on the 1950 Census, throw out the "natives" as not being civilized, throw out the military and their dependents as not part of the permanent population, throw out the government employees as being only transients, and come up with figures that indicated we had virtually no population at all!

In our efforts to convert the unconvinced, we were greatly aided by a number of dedicated groups—the Federation of Women's Clubs, whose representative, Mrs. Leslie Wright, was a tower of strength in mobilizing the club members in the home States of the recalcitrant Senators. These ladies buzzed around obdurate Senators and Congressmen like angry hornets. Others most helpful were the Jaycees, the Kiwanis Clubs, and the Veterans of Foreign Wars.

On one or two occasions when their continued efforts with a particular Senator appeared unavailing, they would concentrate on an individual known to be a very important backer of a certain Senator. That worked.

In the closing weeks of the 2nd Session of the 85th Congress, we got an unexpected break. Edna Ferber's book: *Ice Palace*, appeared in March of 1958. I had gotten Edna to write this book which followed an acquaintance we had struck up some years before when she utilized a passage from my book: *Mexico And Its Heritage*, published in 1928, as the theme for one of her stories, which later became the title of the book that included that short story. It was entitled: *They Brought Their Women.*

In describing the differences between the early history of North America and Latin America, the former being settled, the latter conquered by people from the Old World, I had written as follows:

> "The diversity between the two cultures south and north of the Rio Grande is sharply discernible in the respective status of their women. *The North American settlers brought their women.* The squaw-man was outcast. The exalted position fo woman in the American ideology dates from the pioneer days of companionate hardship and effort . . . The Aztec female, on the other hand, played the part of handmaiden to the warrior male."

Edna Ferber wrote me that she was going to use this as the title of a short story and did so. Having been an admirer of her fiction for some years, I suggested to her that she ought to write a novel about Alaska, and told her of our problems and our desire for statehood. She became interested and made several trips to Alaska to get the necessary background.

Ice Palace made a strong case, in fiction form, for statehood. Some of the literary critics felt it was not up to her best work but one of them referred to it quite correctly as "the Uncle Tom's Cabin for Alaskan statehood". Thousands who would never have been interested in any of our pro-statehood non-fiction magazine articles, of which I had written several for *Harper's, The Atlantic*

Monthly, Current History, the *New York Times Magazine Section,* etc., did read novels.

In the closing weeks of our statehood drive, scores of people asked me whether I had read "Ice Palace." It was called to the attention of many Congressmen by readers who were also their constituents. I have no doubt that it changed quite a few votes.

In the House, action on the Alaska Statehood Bill, H. R. 7999, was delayed in the Rules Committee owing to the opposition of its

Cartoonist Herblock of the Washington *Post* celebrates the passage of the statehood bill in the House and shows Uncle Sam hopefully watching the legislation approach the Senate.

chairman, Representative Howard Smith, D., of Virginia. When it was brought up on May 21, 1958, as a privileged bill by Representative Wayne Aspinall, D., of Colorado, Chairman of the Committee on Interior and Insular Affairs, several points of order were raised against it by Representative Clarence Cannon, D., of Missouri, considered the House's leading parliamentarian.[1]

Other points of order were raised by Representatives Howard Smith and John Taber, R., of New York. But Speaker Rayburn, saying that he had anticipated this action and had made a study of the precedents, overruled the points of order and the motion to bring up the bill prevailed by a vote of 217 to 172.

The debate lasted three days. The statehood case was presented by Representative Leo W. O'Brien, D., of New York, Chairman of the Subcommittee on Territories, the opposition by Representative Arthur Lewis Miller, R., of Nebraska. A motion to recommit by Rep. John Pillion, R., of New York, was defeated 202 to 172, and the bill passed on May 28th, 210 to 166, with 51 not voting.

In the Senate, the statehood bill came up on Monday, June 23rd. There had been some previous proddings for action, notably in a major speech by Frank Church, D., of Idaho, on May 5th with supporting colloquies by Neuberger, D. of Ore.; Thye, R. of Minn.; Carroll, D. of Colo.; Case, R. of North Dakota; Proxmire, D. of Wisconsin; Kennedy, D. of Mass.; Anderson, D. of New Mexico; Yarborough, D. of Texas. In the debate, opened by Senator Murray, D. of Montana, strong support was voiced also by Chavez, D. of New Mexico; Mansfield, D. of Montana; Kuchel, R. of Calif.; Kefauver, D. of Tenn.; Payne, R. of Maine; Holland, D. of Fla.; Pastore, D. of R. I.; Humphrey, D. of Minn.; Allott, R. of Colo.; Douglas, D. of Ill.; Goldwater, R. of Ariz.; Watkins, R. of Utah; Symington, D. of Mo.; Magnuson, D. of Wash.; and Cotton, R. of New Hampshire. Opposition was expressed by Eastland, D. and Stennis, D. of Miss.; Robertson, D. of Va.; Smathers, D. of Fla.; Bush, R. of Conn.; Monroney, D. of Okla. Senator Jackson, D. of Washington, was floor manager of the bill.

The debate went on intermittently for a week. On June 30th various attempts to defeat the bill, by amendment and tactical moves were defeated. A motion by Senator Monroney to substitute Commonwealth status was defeated 50-29. Two points of order raised by Senator Eastland were rejected 53-28 and 62-22. A motion by Senator Stennis to refer the bill to the Armed Services Committee was defeated 53-31. A motion by Senator Thurmond to exclude from statehood the large northern portion of Alaska stipulated in Section 10 of the bill was beaten 67-16.

It was clear that the statehood proponents had an overwhelming majority. When it came up in the evening for a final vote, several who had sought to defeat or sidetrack the bill by amendments, conscious of the historic import of their vote, switched to support it. The vote on passage on June 30, 1958, was 64 yeas, 20 nays, 12 not voting.

There was resounding applause in the galleries which was only mildly rebuked by the presiding officer, Senator Richard Neuberger, long a vigorous statehood supporter.

Final vote on Alaska Statehood Bill (H. R. 7999) June 30, 1958:

Voting "Yea" (64)

Democrats

Clinton Anderson
Alan Bible
John A. Carroll
Dennis Chavez
Frank F. Church
Joseph S. Clark
Paul Douglas
J. Allen Frear
Theodore F. Green
Carl Hayden
Thomas C. Hennings, Jr.
Lister Hill
Spessard Holland
Hubert H. Humphrey
Henry M. Jackson
B. Everett Jordan
Estes Kefauver
John F. Kennedy
Robert Kerr
Frank Lausche
Russell Long

Warren G. Magnuson
Mike Mansfield
Pat McNamara
Wayne Morse
James E. Murray
Richard Neuberger
John O. Pastore
William Proxmire
John Sparkman
Stuart Symington

Republicans

George D. Aiken
Gordon Allott
Frank A. Barrett
Wallace Bennett
John W. Bricker
Homer Capehart
Frank Carlson
Clifford P. Case
Francis H. Case
Norris Cotton

Everett Dirksen
Henry C. Dworshak
Barry Goldwater
Bourke B. Hickenlooper
Roman L. Hruska
Jacob K. Javits
William F. Knowland
Thomas H. Kuchel
William Langer
Thomas E. Martin
Thruston Morton
Karl Mundt
Frederick G. Payne
Charles A. Potter
William A. Purtell
William C. Revercomb
Margaret C. Smith
Howard Alexander Smith
Edward J. Thye
Arthur V. Watkins
Alexander Wiley
John J. Williams
Milton R. Young

Voting "Nay" (20)

Democrats:

Harry F. Byrd
James O. Eastland
Allen J. Ellender
Sam J. Ervin, Jr.
J. William Fulbright
Olin Johnston
John L. McClellan
A. S. Mike Monroney
A. Willis Robertson
Richard B. Russell
John Stennis
Herman E. Talmadge
Strom Thurmond

Republicans:

Styles Bridges
Prescott Bush
John M. Butler
John Sherman Cooper
Edward Martin
Leverett Saltonstall
Andrew F. Schoeppel

Those "not voting" (12)

Democrats:

Albert Gore

Lyndon B. Johnson
Joseph C. O'Mahoney
George A. Smathers
Ralph Yarborough

Republicans:

J. Glenn Beall
Carl T. Curtis
Ralph E. Flanders
John D. Hoblitzell
Irving M. Ives
William E. Jenner
George W. Malone

A small group of Alaskans in the Senate gallery had followed the voting with rapt attention. In addition to Bob and Vide Bartlett were the three of us of the Alaska-Tennessee delegation, Neva and Bill Egan, Martha and Ralph Rivers, Dorothy and Ernest Gruening; Mary Lee Council and Margery Goding Smith, from Bob Bartlett's office; and coming from Alaska to witness this crowning episode in our long struggle, Hugh Wade and Felix Toner from Ju-

Cartoonist Burris Jenkins of the Hearst newspapers pictures the triumph of statehood with passage of the bill in the Senate on June 30, 1958.

neau, the Hinckels from Kodiak, the Noel Wiens from Fairbanks. Jack Hinckel and Ada Wien had been delegates to the Constitutional Convention. It was Ada Wien—born in Nome—who suggested, after the first minutes of elation, that we pray; and together we went to the little non-sectarian chapel in the Capitol, where Ada offered some moving and appropriate words of thanksgiving and of dedication and hope for the success of our future State.

For we were not yet a State! A last ditch effort by the opposition had provided that at the primary election on the following August 26th, when the two political parties would nominate their candidates for the State offices, the people of Alaska should also vote on three propositions: (1) Shall Alaska be admitted to the Union as a State! (2) Shall the boundaries of the new State, as prescribed by the Statehood Act, be approved? (3) Shall all the other provisions of the Act be approved?

If the voters were to reject any one of these propositions, statehood would be defeated and the action of the Congress nullified. But they were overwhelmingly approved, the first of these by 40,452 to 7,010, and the other two by similar majorities.

One final act would complete the statehood process. It took place the following January 3rd, when, at the White House, with Vice President Richard Nixon at his right, Speaker Sam Rayburn at his left, and the Alaska Congressional delegation—Bartlett, Gruening, Rivers—looking over his shoulder, President Eisenhower signed the proclamation making Alaska the 49th State!

*   *   *

Footnotes

INTRODUCTION

1. This little known episode deserves recalling. On February 24, 1941, the twenty-ninth day of the Fifteenth Territorial Legislature, House Bill No. 60 was introduced by Representative William A. Egan of the Third Division and Representative John McCormick of the First Division. It was referred to the Committee on Judiciary and Federal Relations, consisting of Almer J. Peterson, of the Third Division, Jesse D. Lander and Charles F. Herbert, of the Fourth Division, Howard Lyng, of the Second Division, and James V. Davis, of the First Division, who reported it with a "Do Pass" recommendation. It passed the House on March 1 by a vote of 12 to 4. Those voting "aye" were: Davis, Egan, Frank S. Gordon, Herbert, Crystal Snow Jenne, Lander, Lyng, McCormick, Harvey J. Smith, Stuart L. Stangroom, Frank H. Whaley, and H. H. McCutcheon, the Speaker.

The bill was referred to the Senate, where, after a second reading, it was moved by Leroy Sullivan, of the Second Division, seconded by C. H. LaBoyteaux, of the Fourth Division, that it be indefinitely postponed, which it was by a vote of 6 to 2. Those voting "aye" were Norman R. Walker, of the First Division, O. D. Cochran and Leroy Sullivan, of the Second Division, C. H. LaBoyteaux and Hjalmar Nordale, of the Fourth Division. Those voting "nay" were Don Carlos Brownell and H. H. McCutcheon, of the Third Division.

Thus died an earlier effort to ascertain how the people of Alaska felt on statehood

CHAPTER I

1. Two metropolitan papers, however, supported statehood strongly. They were the Anchorage Times, whose editor and publisher was Robert B. Atwood, and the Ketchikan Chronicle, whose editor and publisher was William L. Baker.

2. It was so declared by Senator Andrew Nerland, recognized as Alaska's senior statesman, who, on the session's last night, added: "The Nineteenth Legislative Assembly did what eighteen previous legislatures were unable to do."

3. I had attended the biennial conferences of the Governors of the Western States since 1945, which took place at other seasons, had presented the Alaska statehood case to them, and they were already converted.

CHAPTER III

1. The other members of the full committee not on the subcommittee were: Republicans—Robert F. Rockwell, Colorado; Frank A. Barrett, Wyoming; Wesley A. D'Ewart, Montana. Democrats—Andrew L. Somers, New York; John R. Murdock, Arizona; John A. Carroll, Colorado.

CHAPTER IV

1. Delegate Bartlett's position was based on his belief that adoption of the Miller amendment would jeopardize the enactment of the bill. Addressing the House on March 3, 1950, he said:

"I would like to say to the gentleman from Nebraska that I have a very sympathetic interest in the amendment which he proposes. Actually, Alaska would like to get half of the public land. I was in Alaska last summer and no one talked to me about this particular provision in the statehood bill. As the gentleman knows, there were strong representations made that the executive branch of Government would oppose this provision strongly. Therefore, because I thought the new State could subsist on four sections, I agreed to go along with that provision."

2. Bartlett's letter to Secretary Krug was written on Feb. 22, 1949, over a year earlier.

3. Mr. Arnold's figure was in error. With four sections out of every township which H. R. 331 provided, the Federal Government would retain about 88 and not 99 per cent of the land.

4. Mr. Arnold was correct in regard to H. R. 206's provision, as drafted to Delegate Bartlett's specifications, giving Alaska all the vacant and unappropriated land. This provision, however, encountered the opposition, deemed insuperable, of the Dept. of the Interior, whose objections were expressed in a letter dated April 14, 1947, to Richard J. Welch, Chairman of the House Committee on Public Lands, signed by Warner W. Gardner, Acting Secretary of the Interior, who voiced his opposition in the following terms:

"The public lands provisions to which I have referred are contained in sections 3, 4 and 5 of the bill. I have serious objections to these sections of the bill. H. R. 206, with a few exceptions, would transfer to the new State title to the public lands located in Alaska. This is contrary to the traditional practice which has been followed throughout the West when new States have been admitted to the Union. The custom has been for the Federal Government to grant to the new States lands for schools and for internal improvements, but to retain the bulk of the public lands under Federal ownership. I strongly recommend that there be no change in this practice in the case of Alaska. The Public lands in the Territory were purchased by the United States for the benefit of the Nation as a whole and are, in effect, held in trust for the people of the United States. Congress, as the ultimate manager of the property of all the people, should not turn it over to the relatively few who live in Alaska to use as a source of revenue. Not only would the people of the United States be deprived of their property, but also there would be no assurance that the land and its resources would be developed prudently or in accordance with national needs, nor that the land would be made available to settlers from the other States. Instead, it could be sold in large tracts to a few individuals in order to produce revenue for the State.

"In Line with the preceding comments, I recommend the inclusion in H. R. 206 of provisions which would permit Alaska to enter into the Union on a basis similar to that on which the western continental States were admitted. While retaining the greater part of the public lands for national management the Federal Government has made grants to the new States for school purposes and internal improvements. Similar grants should be made in the case of Alaska.

"Specifically, I recommend grants which would allow Alaska over 21,000,000 acres for the support of its common schools, over 438,000 acres for the support of its agricultural college and school of mines, and 500,000 acres for other internal improvements. This is a far greater amount of public lands than any other State has been given upon its admission."

In consequence of the Interior Dept.'s opposition, H. R. 206 was never reported by the Subcommittee, and Delegate Bartlett introduced H. R. 331 in its stead.

Chapter V

1. These are found on pp. 448-460 of the hearing.

2. Four years previous to this statement, General Eisenhower had declined my invitation to join my nationwide Committee of a Hundred favoring statehood, but expressed his wholehearted sympathy for the cause, basing his declination on a self-imposed rule not to lend his name to committees.

3. Of course she was right. E. G.

Chapter VI

1. The inspiration for this far-sighted and audacious move originated with Wendell P. Kay, an Anchorage attorney who was Speaker of the House. In the previous (1953) legislature, he had sponsored a bill calling for a Constitutional Convention, the ratification of a State constitution, and the election of State officers, with the sponsorship of the other three Democrats in the House: Richard J. Greuel, of Fairbanks; Theodore D. Duffield, of Nome; and Charles E. Fagerstrom, of Nome. The 1953 legislature, swept in by the 1952 Eisenhower tide, also had an 11 to 5 Republican majority in the Senate. Kay's House Bill #7 was referred to a special House Committee on Statehood, where it was promptly interred with a "do not pass" verdict rendered by its 5 Republican members: Howard W. Pollock, of Anchorage; William K. Boardman, of Ketchikan; Carl T. Rentschler, of Anchorage; John B. Coghill, of Nenana; and Frederick O. Estaugh, of Juneau. The 1954 election reversed the political composition of the 1953 legislature and gave the 1955 legislature a 12 to 4 Democratic preponderance in the Senate, and a 21 to 3 margin in the House. All 21 Democrats co-sponsored House Bill #1.

The legislators who enacted this historic legislation in 1955 for a Constitutional Convention were:

House: E. G. Bailey, (D) of Anchorage; Lester Bronson, (D) of Nome; Seaborn J. Buckalew, (D) of Anchorage; Charles E. Fagerstrom, (D) of Nome; Hubert A. Gilbert, (D) of Fairbanks; Richard J. Greuel, (D) of Fairbanks; Ken C. Johnson, (D) of Anchorage; Peter J. Kalamarides, (D) of Anchorage; Ed Locken, (R) of Petersburg; Stanley J. McCutcheon, (D) of Anchorage; Joseph A. McLean, (R) of Juneau; George B. McNabb, Jr., (D) of Fairbanks; Robert J. McNealy, (D) of Fairbanks; Vernon M. Metcalfe, (D) of Juneau; Harry B. Palmer, (D) of Anchorage; Raymond E. Plummer, (D) of Anchorage; Burke Riley, (D) of Haines; Irene E. Ryan, (D) of Anchorage; Thomas B. Stewart, (D) of Juneau; Dora M. Sweeney, (D) of Juneau; Warren A. Taylor, (D) of Fairbanks; Russell K. Young, (D) of Anchorage; Wendell P. Kay, (D) of Anchorage.

Opposed: Edith R. Bullock, (R) of Kotzebue.

Senate: Doris M. Barnes, (R) of Wrangell; Frank Barr, (D) of Fairbanks; William E. Beltz, (D) of Nome; John Butrovich, (R) of Fairbanks; J. Earl Cooper, (D) of Anchorage; William A. Egan,

(D) of Valdez; R. E. Ellis, (D) of Ketchikan; Neal W. Foster, (D) of Nome; Charles D. Jones, (R) of Nome; Howard Lyng, (D) of Nome; Marcus Jensen, (D) of Douglas; James Nolan, (D) of Wrangell; Al Owen, (D) of Anchorage; Ralph J. Rivers, (D) of Fairbanks; Mike Stepovich, (R) of Fairbanks; and J. H. Werner, (D) of Seward.
(Journal of the Senate, 1955, p. 460)

2. The members of the Constitutional Convention were:

The Rev. R. Rolland Armstrong, Juneau, Presbyterian minister (later President of Sheldon Jackson Junior College in Sitka)

Miss Dorothy J. Awes, Palmer; lawyer.

Frank Barr, Fairbanks; bush pilot, Territorial legislator.

John C. Boswell, Fairbanks; Manager of Operations of the U. S. Smelting, Refining & Mining Company.

Seaborn J. Buckalew, Jr., Anchorage; lawyer, Territorial Legislator.

John B. Coghill, Nenana; merchant, Territorial legislator.

E. B. Collins, Harding Lake; retired lawyer, Territorial legislator.

George D. Cooper, Fairbanks; owner of a ready-mix concrete business.

John M. Cross, Kotzebue; bush pilot.

Edward V. Davis, Anchorage; lawyer.

James P. Doogan, Fairbanks; trucker and mover.

William A. Egan, Valdez; merchant, Territorial legislator (later Governor of Alaska).

Truman C. Emberg, Dillingham; commercial fisherman and union official.

Mrs. Helen Fischer, Anchorage; housewife and Democratic Party official.

Victor Fischer, Anchorage; city planner.

Douglas Gray, Juneau; former Fish & Wildlife Service agent, hotel manager, Territorial legislator.

Thomas C. Harris, Valdez; businessman.

Mrs. Mildred R. Hermann, Juneau; lawyer, had served as Alaska Director of the Office of Price Administration during World War II and was active in women's club affairs.

Herb Hilscher, Anchorage; public relations, author.

Jack Hinckel, Kodiak; land consignee for Union Oil Company.

James Hurley, Palmer; manager of the Alaska Rural Rehabilitation Corporation.

Maurice T. Johnson, Fairbanks; lawyer, Territorial legislator.

Yule F. Kilcher, Homer; homesteader and rancher.

Leonard H. King, Haines; merchant.

William W. Knight, Sitka; merchant, had been Superintendent of the Alaska Pioneers' Home.

W. W. Laws, Nome; Chief of Police, Territorial legislator.

Eldor R. Lee, Petersburg; commercial fisherman.

The Rev. Maynard D. Londborg, Unalakleet; Swedish Covenant missionary.

Steve McCutcheon, Anchorage; photo shop owner, Territorial legislator.

George M. McLaughlin, Anchorage; lawyer.

Robert J. McNealy, Fairbanks; lawyer, Territorial legislator.

John A. McNees, Nome; businessman and former Weather Bureau employee, Territorial legislator.

M.R. Marston, Anchorage; realtor; had organized Alaska Territorial Guard in World War II.

Irwin L. Metcalf, Seward; merchant; had served as Deputy Marshal.

Leslie Nerland, Fairbanks; merchant.

James Nolan, Wrangell; druggist, Territorial legislator.

Mrs. Katherine D. Nordale, Juneau; bank employee, former Collector of Customs for Alaska.

Frank Peratrovich, Klawock; merchant and fisherman, Territorial legislator.

Chris Poulsen, Anchorage; theatre owner.

Peter L. Reader, Nome; businessman.

Burke Riley, Haines; lawyer, formerly Administrative Assistant to the Governor, and Territorial legislator.

Ralph J. Rivers, Fairbanks; lawyer, former U. S. Attorney, Territorial legislator, Territorial Attorney General, Mayor of Fairbanks, member of Unemployment Compensation Commission (later member of U. S. House of Representatives).

Victor C. Rivers, Anchorage; architect and engineer, Territorial legislator.

R. E. Robertson, Juneau; lawyer.

John H. Rosswog, Cordova; druggist.

B. D. Stewart, Sitka; retired Territorial Commissioner of Mines.

W. O. Smith, Ketchikan; commercial fisherman.

George Sundborg, Juneau; newspaper editor, served as Executive Assistant to the Governor and as General Manager of the Alaska Development Board.

Mrs. Dora M. Sweeney, Juneau; housewife, Territorial legislator.

Warren A. Taylor, Fairbanks; lawyer, Territorial legislator.

H. R. Vander Leest, Juneau; retired druggist.

M. J. Walsh, Nome; miner and businessman.

Barrie M. White, Anchorage; businessman.

Mrs. Ada B. Wien, Fairbanks; housewife.

3. In a public address at Denver, September 16, 1950, General Dwight D. Eisenhower declared: "Quick admission of Alaska and Hawaii to statehood will show the world that America practices what it preaches."

Chapter VII
1. Hearings, 84th Congr., 1st Sess., p. 22.

Chapter VIII
1. Cannon was the author of several authoritative textbooks and manuals on House procedure and precedents.

INDEX

Abernethy, Rep. Thomas G., 43
Abood, Mitchel, 68
Absentee interests, in Alaska, 1-2, 9, 15, 17, 18, 19, 23, 81
Adams, Jerry, 65
Agriculture, in Alaska, 34-35
Aiken, Senator George D., 55, 105
Air Commerce Act of 1926, 87
Air transportation, 87-88
Alaska: administration of justice, 28-30, 76; importance for national defense, 48, 54; representation in Congress, Introduction, 3, 9, 27, 36, 77; revenue, 1, 3, 10; revenue, need for, 1-3, 56; territorial status, compared to that of colonies, Prologue, 74-91, 96-97, see also, Territorial status
Alaska, statehood for: bills in Congress, 43-44, 55-57; Congressional hearings, 1947, 14-17; 1950, 44-55; 1957-59, 95-97; Congressional hearings, in Alaska, 1947, 17-41; 1953, 60-69; creation of a national committee, 13-14; early efforts, Introduction
Alaska Airlines, 16, 19
Alaska Bill, S. 50, The, 60
Alaska Coast Guard, see U.S. Coast Guard
Alaska Highway, 85
Alaska Peninsula, 37
Alaska Salmon Industry, 20-21, 50, 52
Alaska Statehood Association, 9, 18
Alaska statehood bill (H.R. 206), 14, 16, 43, 52-54, 108-109
Alaska statehood bill (H.R. 331), 43-44, 47, 48, 52-55, 57, 109
Alaska statehood bill (H.R. 7999), 103-105
Alaska statehood bills, Congressional attempts to defeat, 55-56, 57, 104-105, 106
Alaska Statehood Committee, 10-12, 72, 99
Alaska Steamship Company, 19, 32, 84
Alaska-Tennessee delegation, Introduction, 72, 73, 101, 105
"Alaska-Tennessee Plan", Introduction, 72, 95, 101
Alaska Transportation Co., 32

Alaska Visitors' Association, 84
Albrecht, Dr. Earl, 22
Aleutians, 40, 98
Alewine, Millard Fillmore, 68
Alfsen, Rev. Victor, 64
Allen, Edward W., 54
Allen, Rep. John J., Jr., 32
Allen, Riley H., 61
Allott, Senator Gordon, 104, 105
Almquist, G. E., 10
Anchorage, 2, 9, 17, 18-20, 21, 28, 29, 47, 66-69, 94
Anchorage Times, 11, 16, 42, 52, 99, 107
Anderson, Abel, 10
Anderson, Al, 20
Anderson, Dr. Charles, 67
Anderson, Senator Clinton P., 44, 45, 46, 48, 54, 55, 60, 62, 64, 69, 104, 105
Anderson, Edward, 10
Angell, Rep. Homer D., 14, 32, 43
Angerman, Frank, 10, 21
Angoon, 34
Antarctic expedition, 1938, Prologue
Antarctica, 52
Arctic Circle, 40, 94
Armstrong, Rev. R. Rolland, 19, 51, 110
Arn, Governor Edward F., 8
Arnall, Ellis, 13
Arnold, Gen. H. H., 13, 14
Arnold, W. C., 20-21, 52-54, 108
Ashby, Joe H., 63
Aspinall, Rep. Wayne, 43, 104
Atwood, Evangeline, 9, 18-19, 52
Atwood, Robert B., 9, 11, 12, 16, 52, 99, 107
Avakoff, Harry B., 65
Awes, Miss Dorothy J., 110

Baker, William L., 9, 11, 15, 23, 46, 107
Bakkem, Chris, 61
Bailey, E. G., 69, 109
Baldwin, Ed, 69
Baltzo, C. Howard, 22-23
Banfield, Norman, 63
Barkley, Vice-President Alben, 55
Barnes, Doris, 10, 109
Barr, Frank, 10, 109, 110
Barrett, Frank A.: as Representative, 107; as Senator, 60, 95, 96, 105

5/21/62

DATE DUE
